Leading with a Whisper is a powerful testament to the unwavering faith and courage of a woman who has dedicated her life to serving God and advocating for the vulnerable. Beth Grant's story is a beacon of hope, reminding us that God's strength is made perfect in our weakness. Her journey will inspire leaders, ministers, and believers to step into their callings with boldness and compassion. This book is a must-read for anyone seeking to understand the heart of God for His daughters and the transformative power of obedience to His call.

—JOHN L. EASTER, PHD
EXECUTIVE DIRECTOR, ASSEMBLIES OF GOD
WORLD MISSIONS

In *Leading with a Whisper*, Beth Grant offers us a priceless window into the journey of a quiet and serious little girl with a deep desire to follow Jesus whatever the cost or consequences. Despite the painful heartbreak of widowhood at the age of twenty-five, her covenantal resolve to keep following Jesus even though "none go with" her became the doorway to an unbelievable adventure with Jesus. It led to several milestone achievements: a powerful teaching and preaching ministry that impacted three continents, creating history as the first woman to serve on the Executive Presbytery of the Assemblies of God USA, and cofounding with her husband Project Rescue, a ministry that today provides healing and hope for victims of sex trafficking in forty-two cities across sixteen nations. This book is vintage Beth

Grant—honest, transparent, and God honoring—but it is especially compelling because it is not just her story. It is an invitation to learn from an iconic, passionately devoted follower of Jesus how you, the reader, can also experience what it means to have Beth's Jesus write a chapter of His story through your life.

—Ivan Satyavrata, PhD
Board Chair, World Vision International;
Pastor Emeritus, The Assembly of God
Church, Kolkata

The Assemblies of God has been blessed by the ministry and leadership of God's gifted daughters. I am so thankful that in our generation God brought an anointed leader whose life and influence have had a profound impact. Thank you, Beth, for modeling what Scripture supports, that God raises up daughters and sons for spiritual leadership and kingdom expansion through the local church.

—Rev. Doug Clay
General Superintendent, Assemblies of
God USA

Whenever I spend time with Beth Grant, I walk away with a glimpse of Jesus. This book is no exception. You will continually find yourself gazing at the glory of Jesus through a surrendered life. *Leading with a Whisper* beautifully reflects on the life of an ordinary woman who entrusted herself to an extraordinary God. Through telling her story, Beth's prophetic voice will continue to lead generations to come, as they choose to follow the Spirit through the unknowns, and not turn back.

—STEPHANIE NANCE, DMIN
LEAD PASTOR, CHAPEL SPRINGS CHURCH

This heart-moving book is more than just an autobiography. It is a classic case study in how the lives of groundbreaking influencers are forged and formed. Beth has been a longtime friend. I have seen her sit at the table of top-level leadership, watched her minister in the prophetic power of the Spirit, and gotten to know the amazing family that she has raised. Thankfully, she has decided to write her story for the benefit of the rest of us. Read it with gratefulness—it promises to instruct and inspire your own journey.

—JAMES BRADFORD, PHD
LEAD PASTOR, CENTRAL ASSEMBLY OF GOD,
SPRINGFIELD, MISSOURI;
FORMER GENERAL SECRETARY, GENERAL
COUNCIL OF THE ASSEMBLIES OF GOD

For many of us in the Assemblies of God, Rev. Dr. Beth Grant is a giant of ministry, a hero to generations of women who have watched her lead so well. In this book we get an inside view of the life and calling of this amazing woman who, despite her own personality and quiet demeanor, has a roar inside her that is released by the power and anointing of the Holy Spirit. In *Leading with a Whisper*, Beth chronicles her life shaped by a love for God, a long obedience in the same direction, and the faithfulness of the God who called her to follow Him in all things. Throughout the narrative of love, loss, triumph, and tragedy, Rev. Grant reminds her reader that none of these moments were without the presence of the Spirit. While Beth may not have sought a stage, a spotlight, or even a voice, God has given her a place of leadership for women from the brothels of South Asia to the highest offices of the Assemblies of God worldwide. Beth is a mentor and a mother in the faith to women like me, who are called to lead, who need to see in the flesh what God has called us to be. Her highest calling, however, remains to be a disciple of Jesus, and throughout the book she returns to this great call time and again. And in only the way He can, the God who calls is faithful to His daughters; His girl Beth is a grand witness to this truth.

—REV. JOY E. A. QUALLS, PhD
PROFESSOR AND ASSOCIATE DEAN, BIOLA
UNIVERSITY

Beth Grant's *Leading with a Whisper* is an extraordinary book that beautifully blends personal narrative with powerful spiritual insights. Through intimate storytelling and genuine vulnerability Beth invites readers into her own journey of faith, courage, and quiet strength. Her authenticity and humility shine throughout the book, inspiring readers to listen closely for God's voice in their own lives.

Beth's approach to leadership, characterized by

gentle yet unwavering obedience, resonates deeply with readers who seek guidance and clarity in their own spiritual journeys. Her writing conveys warmth, wisdom, and sincere compassion, making readers feel as if they are walking alongside a trusted friend and mentor. Throughout, Beth Grant models authenticity in a way that is refreshing and deeply encouraging. You will be inspired by her steadfast faith, moved by her vulnerability, and challenged by her courageous willingness to follow God's leading—no matter the cost.

—ROD LOY
PASTOR, FIRST ASSEMBLY OF GOD, NORTH LITTLE ROCK, ARKANSAS; AUTHOR, *HELP! I'M IN CHARGE*, *IMMEDIATE OBEDIENCE*, AND *AFTER THE HONEYMOON*

Beth Grant may lead with a whisper, but her ministry as an advocate for sexually trafficked women and children has resulted in loud shouts of praise to God around the world. In this book she tells her story of trusting Jesus through the high and low moments of life. And she urges believers to step in, step up, and step out as the Holy Spirit leads us to take the good news to a spiritually and socially broken world.

—DONNA BARRETT
GENERAL SECRETARY, ASSEMBLIES OF GOD USA

Many people think it sounds like thunder when God speaks. However, Elijah knew it could sound like a still, small wind or voice (1 Kings 19). If you have ever heard Beth Grant speak, you know God can sound like a whisper. Her thoughts and words are powerful. Her thunder comes through in this book as she describes the adventure of an unfolding call to service, sacrifice, and spiritual victory. Her preaching has given credence to women in ministry and women in missions leadership for five decades. Her whispered wisdom has led to seats at many elite tables from Maryland to India. Lean in to her whisper because her words always contain the power of truth. Read and be ready to hear God's voice!

—REV. TERRY RABURN, DMIN
SUPERINTENDENT, PENINSULAR FLORIDA
DISTRICT COUNCIL OF
THE ASSEMBLIES OF GOD

Beth Grant epitomizes gentle strength. Drawing from her own personal journey and prophetic inspiration, she is sure to captivate your heart and mobilize your feet into action. *Leading with a Whisper* is sure to have a ripple effect on sons and daughters for generations to come.

—MELISSA J. ALFARO, PHD
EXECUTIVE PRESBYTER, ASSEMBLIES OF GOD USA;
NATIONAL DIRECTOR, ASSEMBLIES OF GOD
NETWORK OF WOMEN MINISTERS

In *Leading with a Whisper*, Beth Grant shares her deeply personal journey of faith, calling, and courage with the same quiet strength that has defined her life and ministry for decades. I've had the privilege of calling Beth a friend and colleague for over thirty years, and I can confidently say that her integrity, wisdom, and compassion run deep. I have watched her live and lead with passion and excellence. This book is more than a memoir—it's a gentle, Spirit-led invitation to step into the life God calls each of us to live. Beth's story will inspire and challenge you, just as she has inspired and challenged me.

—Kevin Donaldson
Administrator, Assemblies of God World
Missions

A life lived consecrated to serve God no matter the cost, the level of comfort, the unfathomable atrocities of evil around her, or the sheer amount of obstacles in front of her—that is the life into which Beth Grant grants us glimpses in her book *Leading with a Whisper*. While reading, you will understand that this was not what she had in mind or would have considered possible. But *God* saw so much more, took what she offered, and spiced it with an extra ingredient called David Grant. And an adventure of living out her calling unfolded. But if you expect only stories, you need to be warned. Beth Grant's whisper carries a strong apostolic authority, speaking into society's and our zeitgeist's injustice, apathy, and spiritual darkness. You will be challenged. Her wisdom that was whispered into my life had a lasting and much louder prophetic impact on my ministry and the future God had for me. This book continues to do exactly that

again for me now, and I am convinced it will for you too as you read.
—RUTH HASSELGREN GRIESFELDER
PASTOR, PINGSTKYRKAN ESKILSTUNA;
COORDINATOR FOR EUROPEAN MISSIONS,
PINGST, SWEDEN

Leading with a Whisper by Beth Grant is a must-read for a generation that may feel unfit or unlikely to be chosen by God for ministry. Having had the privilege of learning from Beth and serving alongside her in Project Rescue, I've witnessed her wisdom, unwavering obedience, and Spirit-led tenacity, all beautifully captured in this book. For the first time, she shares her faith journey with heartfelt vulnerability, revealing her struggles, lessons, and the powerful moments of God's faithfulness throughout. With quiet strength and an authentic voice Beth's book is more than just an autobiography—it's a road map to leading with bold faith, complete surrender, and spiritual courage.
—RAEGAN GLUGOSH
NORTH ATLANTIC AND CANADA AREA
DIRECTOR, ASSEMBLIES OF GOD WORLD
MISSIONS

Beth Grant's powerful, prophetic voice is a gift to the church. Those that know of Project Rescue or who have heard her preach and teach will be inspired and encouraged as she describes how God taught a quiet, reflective young woman to be a Spirit-sensitive, Spirit-led leader who listens to His still, small voice and obeys with supernatural courage. *Leading with a*

Whisper will draw you in with stories of life and ministry and will challenge you with words of wisdom and passionate conviction. By God's grace Rev. Grant has used her voice to call people to freedom in Christ and to give voice to multiplied thousands whose stories would never have been heard. Watching that unfold through the pages of this book will inspire any Christian leader and follower of Christ.

—DAVID J. KIM, DMIN
PRESIDENT, UNIVERSITY OF VALLEY FORGE

Beth Grant, the first woman to serve as an executive presbyter of the Assemblies of God fellowship and the founder of the Network of Women Ministers, has inspired a generation of women to embrace their ministerial calling and break through the leadership barriers that were once reserved for men. She is a skilled leader who exemplifies excellence and preparedness. However, her commitment to corporate intercession, her prophetic voice guided by the Holy Spirit, and her compassion for those often overlooked by society have truly empowered generations to come. *Leading with a Whisper* offers readers an insightful look into the life of this influential global leader. Beth has motivated a generation to pursue prophetic, Spirit-led servant leadership through her whispered message. May her intimate life story encourage you to answer the same call.

—REV. CRYSTAL MARTIN
DIRECTOR (2017–2024), NETWORK OF WOMEN
MINISTERS;
GLOBAL WORKER TO NORTHERN EUROPE,
ASSEMBLIES OF GOD WORLD MISSIONS

Leading with a Whisper is a must-read. Beth Grant's deeply personal and prophetic journey challenges and inspires emerging leaders to embrace the quiet yet powerful call of God. With authenticity and vulnerability Beth traces her path through moments of faith, calling, sacrifice, and global impact—all illuminated by a divine whisper she received in a dark night of pain: "Step in. Step up. Step out." Each chapter, from her tender beginnings in faith to her transformative work in India to advocating for women in ministry, offers insights into spiritual leaders who are marked by humility, courage, and obedience. I encourage every leader and follower of Jesus to imitate Beth's example, to lead not with a shout but with a whisper empowered by God.

—Pastor Mark Lehmann
Cornerstone Church

In a world clamoring for attention, this book invites us into something deeper: to soak in God's presence so fully that when we speak, it is His voice people hear. Beth Grant has spent her life leaning in, led by the whisper of the Spirit—and countless lives have been changed. Her life is a testament that what matters most is not how loud we speak but how closely we are listening to the Spirit. May our voices grow quieter, that His might be heard.

Over a decade ago Beth Grant's "power whisper" helped me hear God's gentle whisper, leading me on the greatest adventure of my life. This book has the power to do the same for you, inviting you to hear God's whisper and embark on your own life-changing journey. As you turn the pages, don't just read—listen. You will hear the whisper of God, and it just might change everything.

—Brianna Petersen
Oasis, Dhaka, Bangladesh

Many Pentecostal gatherings include space for personal testimonies. Anyone in the congregation can stand at an appointed time and testify to what God has done or is doing for them. These testimonies range from stories of dramatic healings and deliverance to summaries of God's faithfulness over the course of a life.

Beth Grant's *Leading with a Whisper* epitomizes a Pentecostal testimony. Rev. Grant is well known throughout the Assemblies of God for her contributions to missions, her leadership in the fight against human trafficking, and her representation of women as the first female executive presbyter. This story, however, is not the story of a great woman but her testimony of a great God!

Rev. Grant narrates the faithfulness of God throughout her story of a life marked by tragedy but led by hope. Readers will be struck by her honest appraisal of a life lived for God. More than that, they will see why such a life is worth living.

—D. Allen Tennison, PhD
Theological Counsel, National Office of
the Assemblies of God

Leading
with a
Whisper

Beth Grant

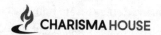

LEADING WITH A WHISPER by Beth Grant
Published by Charisma House, an imprint of Charisma Media
1150 Greenwood Blvd., Lake Mary, Florida 32746

Copyright © 2025 by Beth Grant. All rights reserved.

Unless otherwise noted, all Scripture quotations are taken from the Holy Bible, New International Version®, NIV®. Copyright © 1973, 1978, 1984, 2011 by Biblica, Inc.® Used by permission of Zondervan. All rights reserved worldwide. www.zondervan. com. The "NIV" and "New International Version" are trademarks registered in the United States Patent and Trademark Office by Biblica, Inc.®

Scripture quotations marked ESV are from The ESV® Bible (The Holy Bible, English Standard Version®), copyright © 2001 by Crossway, a publishing ministry of Good News Publishers. Used by permission. All rights reserved.

Scripture quotations marked NASB are taken from the (NASB®) New American Standard Bible®, Copyright © 1960, 1971, 1977, 1995 by The Lockman Foundation. Used by permission. All rights reserved. www.lockman.org

Scripture quotations marked NLT are taken from the *Holy Bible*, New Living Translation, copyright ©1996, 2004, 2015 by Tyndale House Foundation. Used by permission of Tyndale House Publishers, Carol Stream, Illinois 60188. All rights reserved.

Scripture quotations marked NRSVUE are from the New Revised Standard Version, Updated Edition. Copyright © 2021 by the National Council of Churches of Christ in the United States of America. Used by permission. All rights reserved worldwide.

Scripture quotations marked RSV are from the Revised Standard Version of the Bible. Copyright © 1946, 1952, 1971 by the Division of Christian Education of the National Council of the Churches of Christ in the USA. Used by permission.

Scriptures marked WEB are taken from the World English Bible, public domain.

While the author has made every effort to provide accurate, up-to-date source information at the time of publication, statistics and other data are constantly updated. Neither the publisher nor the author assumes any responsibility for errors or for changes that occur after publication. Further, the publisher and author do not have any control over and do not assume any responsibility for third-party websites or their content.

For more resources like this, visit MyCharismaShop.com and the author's website at projectrescue.com.

Cataloging-in-Publication Data is on file with the Library of Congress.
International Standard Book Number: 978-1-63641-406-5
E-book ISBN: 978-1-63641-407-2

1 2025

Printed in the United States of America

Most Charisma Media products are available at special quantity discounts for bulk purchase for sales promotions, premiums, fundraising, and educational needs. For details, call us at (407) 333-0600 or visit our website at charismamedia.com.

The author has made every effort to provide accurate accounts of events, but she acknowledges that others may have different recollections of these events.

Some reflection questions in part 2 were developed with the use of ChatGPT (and subsequently edited for content), OpenAI, March 18, 2025, https://chatgpt.com/.

To dear David, who joyfully and lovingly welcomed me into his heart, his world, and his passionate journey to preach Jesus to the nations.

To Mom and Dad, Rebecca and Tyler, and Jennifer and Jon, who have walked so closely, been sources of strength and joy, and shared in the sacrifices of my yes to Jesus.

To God's daughters near and far who have heard God whisper their names—His hand is upon you, His gifts are within you, His fire burns in your souls, and you discern the wind of His Spirit blowing. Keep stepping in, stepping up, and stepping out in faith and power as God leads.

"The one who calls you is faithful, and he will do it" (1 Thess. 5:24).

To the only One who holds my life in His hands—You have always been faithful. You covered me with Your presence, spoke softly in my quiet places, stirred a fire in my soul, and strengthened my hands and voice for battle—epic battles that must be fought and won in Jesus' powerful name so beloved captives can be set free!

To You, O Lord, in all things—all glory, honor, and praise be unto You!

Contents

Foreword by Byron D. Klaus xxi

Preface... xxiii

Part I
Foundations of Leadership

Chapter 1   A Tender, Feisty Faith........................ 1

Chapter 2   An Unfolding Call........................... 14

Chapter 3   No Turning Back 23

Chapter 4   God's Gift of David.........................30

Chapter 5   India Captured My Heart 41

Chapter 6   Different Kinds of Sowing...................50

Part II
Navigating Change and Growth

Chapter 7   Harems, Servant Leaders, and Little Kings..... 63

Chapter 8   Breaking Ground for Hope 75

Chapter 9   A Voice for God's Daughters..................93

Chapter 10   A Seat at the Table........................109

Chapter 11   No Turning Back (Reprise) 127

Chapter 12   Lord of Our Seasons 138

A Personal Invitation to Know Jesus.................. 152

Appendix A: Practical Ways to Mentor Children to Act Compassionately Toward Victims of Exploitation...153

LEADING WITH A WHISPER

Appendix B: The Role of Women in Ministry as Described in Holy Scripture 155

Appendix C: Recommended Reading List ...,......167

Notes 171

Acknowledgments 173

About the Author 176

Contact Us 178

Foreword

For those of us who have long admired the ministry of Beth Grant, we now have the rest of the story. Through this telling of her life journey you will come to understand the foundation of her prophetic voice. Her spiritual authority and influence, which I have observed, have come from a lifetime of obedience in the unseen moments of her life that reflect an ordinariness as well as tragedy.

The voice of Beth Grant has sounded a clarion call in her advocacy for women in ministry, as well as for the disenfranchised women and children in poverty. But she is no crusader as contemporary culture would understand it; rather, she is a faithful follower of Jesus empowered by the Spirit to proclaim the good news of Jesus Christ with spiritual authority and trustworthiness.

While the life and ministry of Beth Grant certainly must be described as extraordinary, they are also a template for all who follow Jesus. Obedience to the call of God on our lives is met by the Holy Spirit of Pentecost, which falls on both women and men to carry the continuing mission of Jesus Christ to the places where it is most resisted and least accessible.

Leading with a Whisper is a peek into the life of a faithful servant who has heard God speak in the valley of the shadow of death and on the mountaintop of victory. Beth Grant's life is a testimony to a long obedience in the same direction.

—Byron D. Klaus, DMin
President (1999–2015), Assemblies of God
Theological Seminary

Preface

IF I AM remembered for anything I said from a platform in my life, it will likely be eight minutes at an Assemblies of God (AG) Influence Conference in Orlando in 2019. It was a moment for my husband, David, and me that our Assemblies of God leadership graciously planned without our knowledge. At the end of the beautiful presentation, David expressed our deep appreciation and then passed the microphone to me.

Unbeknownst to anyone in the audience, five months before that I had been recovering from major surgery. In the middle of the night with David beside me, I was in pain and trying unsuccessfully to sleep. Suddenly, God's presence was powerfully close, and I heard Him speak six strong words to me: "Step in! Step up! Step out!"

God's presence and His words were so strong and unmistakable that tears ran down my cheeks in the dark. With all my heart I prayed, "I hear You, Lord. I do. And I will do what You are asking."

But I sensed God's words were not just for me. My mind raced through the ministry platform events scheduled for the months ahead. None of them seemed to be the audience for whom this message was intended. But God's presence was reassuring. "Trust Me. You'll know."

Five months later in a moment at the Influence Conference that no one could have orchestrated, the mic was handed to me with a question: "Beth, if there was one thing you would want to share with a younger generation who is following you in ministry, what would it be?"

I looked out at the faces of a thousand younger men and women whom God deeply loves and who were desperately

xxiii

hungry to hear from Him. The weight of the moment was heavy. And I knew.

As I opened my mouth, He spoke powerfully. I realized He had prophetically given me the outline, "Step in. Step up. Step out!" And the words for the message that flowed freely in that holy moment came from my Father. My whisper was overwhelmed by His presence—and I was left in awe, once again, at God's amazing ways as I follow Jesus. His words for a prophetic public moment flowed from a quiet daughter who heard her Father's still, small voice in the dark of night.

Executive presbyter and Project Rescue friend Pastor Rod Loy surprising David and me with the 2019 Influence Lifetime Achievement Award

Our kids and grandkids were all in on the surprise. We were with countless dear friends and respected leaders. It became a very powerful moment in God's presence.

Part I

Foundations *of* Leadership

Chapter 1

A Tender, Feisty Faith

ONE SUNDAY MORNING, a young mother was sitting on the back row of a small Pentecostal church, holding her baby girl on her lap. A guest evangelist preached on the Holy Spirit and then gave a call for prayer for those who were hungry to receive the baptism in the Holy Spirit. The young woman was so hungry for God and all He had for her that even as others went forward, she sat in the back, holding her baby, with tears rolling down her face in God's presence.

Suddenly, the evangelist noted the young mother praying on the back row and pointed to her.

"Sister, you were just baptized in the Holy Spirit! Would you like to share with us what just happened to you?"

The young woman responded with sincerity, "Brother, God has powerfully touched me, and I'm so grateful. But I wasn't baptized with the Spirit this morning. I believe He will baptize me one day, and when He does, I know it will be wonderful."

But the minister insisted, "Sister, yes, you were filled with the Holy Spirit!"

With her baby in her arms the young mother replied respectfully, "Sir, I was not. I've been deeply blessed. But if that was the baptism, I would be disappointed. I'm hungry for the day God will fill me with His Spirit."

Within months, that young woman actually was powerfully filled with the Holy Spirit. She continued to attend the church for fifty-four more years, seeking God with all her heart for what He had promised.

And I was the baby girl the woman with such feisty faith was holding in her arms that day.

⤙⤙⤙⤙⤙

My mom, Eleanor, was the oldest of three children, born to Clayton and Elizabeth Beiswenger Poe in 1923. Her mother died of tuberculosis when Eleanor was only four years old, and her siblings were three and one. As the oldest, Eleanor immediately became the caregiver, an independent little girl who had to be strong to help her siblings and father survive.

With three little ones to raise, her father enlisted family members who could help care for them. By the time he remarried and a stepmother came into the picture, Eleanor had already become a little too strong, independent, and protective to be a "sweet little girl" anymore. She learned to be respectful but make her own way on behalf of her siblings.

At seventeen Mom finished her education, both at high school and at Strayer Business School outside Washington, DC. Her first job was at Riggs National Bank, across the street from the White House. Soon, she had a reputation for being excellent at her work, very professional with a great mind for detail. When the father of Jacqueline Bouvier (later Jacqueline Kennedy) was looking for an executive secretary, a leader at Riggs recommended the young Eleanor Poe. But knowing his reputation as a womanizer, Mom firmly refused his offer.

It was not long before a handsome young man from northern Maine playing a Gibson guitar showed up at Bethel Assembly of God Church in Savage, Maryland. Eleanor quickly caught his eye, and he caught hers too. And the rest is history.

Soon after I was born, my mother started working for

A Tender, Feisty Faith

the government as an executive assistant to a director in the Department of Agriculture. I grew up watching her do a job that up to that point had been done by a man. She was wise, professional, and open about her faith in a very secular, skeptical environment. Mom had to work to help pay the bills. She was simultaneously a devoted wife and mother and a faithful prayer warrior and adult Sunday school teacher at Bethel Assembly. At 101 years of age she is the last remaining charter member of her home church. (And yes, Mom is still a woman of feisty faith.)

My dad was born into a family known for its anger and alcohol on the northern border of Maine, near Canada. His dad, Harden Oakes, was a hard, sometimes violent man who worked the potato farms for a living. He would work for a farmer until his temper got the best of him; then he'd quit, go home, and tell his wife, "Alice, we're moving. Get ready to go." And my grandmother, patient and strong, would pack up their five little children and whatever they had left and get ready to move one more time. It was a very hard life, and my grandfather's anger was a thing to be feared. My grandmother was a saint, but there was nothing she could do but try to placate Harden.

But their oldest child, Hollis, always had a gentle spirit. At fourteen he was unable to handle the family fighting any longer and decided to take his own life. Miraculously, in the process Jesus appeared to him in a vision. And in that moment, Hollis— my dad—determined to love and serve Jesus for the rest of his life. And so he did, from that moment until he died at age eighty-three.

Dad married Mom in 1948 and spent most of his working years as a cashier at local grocery store chains. Customers would wait extra time to be in "Mr. Hollis' line" because he loved people and was so encouraging. If they were struggling, Dad would always assure them he was praying for them. Strangers would

3

LEADING WITH A WHISPER

show up at our door because Mr. Hollis had told them they were welcome to come.

Dad served our home church, Bethel Assembly, for several generations, playing his Gibson guitar or mandolin for worship and kids' church. He had a gift for music and a tender heart for Jesus and worship. When he retired, he went to work full time as janitor for our church's Christian school. When Alzheimer's disease began to take its devastating toll, young nursing assistants would offer to take care of him because he always had a smile; had a gentle, grateful spirit; and loved people.

Each summer, our family made a trip to see Dad's family in Fort Fairfield, Maine. It was always beautiful—and it was always hard. Each visit included lots of laughter because the Oakes family had a great sense of humor. But it also included my grandfather and several of Dad's siblings drinking and mocking Dad constantly for his faith, his convictions, and his tender heart. We were the odd ones out, for sure. At the end of each visit, we'd hug everyone goodbye, and as we headed south for the long drive back to Maryland, not a word would be spoken for the first couple of hours—but I'd see tears quietly streaming down my dad's face.

Dad never gave up praying for his family. He and Mom never stopped making the long journey north every year. Instead, he and Mom loved, cared for, and prayed for his family, their children, and their grandchildren for decades. And over the years, Dad saw his own father, several of his siblings, and some of their children decide to follow Jesus.

God was, is, and will be faithful. My dad and mom were loving and faithful too.

4

A Tender, Feisty Faith

As a child I spent more time alone than most kids my age. My parents both worked, and I was an only child until I was ten, when my baby brother, Tim, was born. So before and after school, an aunt or housekeeper would keep me. I was quiet, always thinking, listening to others, reading, and reflecting.

At five I was diagnosed with rheumatic fever and was bedridden for six months to prevent heart damage. There was no TV for me—only schoolwork to do, encyclopedias to read, time to draw, and a radio to listen to. One program that caught my attention was sponsored by The Leprosy Mission. It was very dramatic, and I was convinced I had leprosy but no one wanted to tell me.

Yes, I was born quiet and serious. I felt a responsibility not to ask for anything I didn't think my parents could afford. New dresses came at Easter and Christmas, and we prayed before shopping that God would help us find something pretty that we could afford. My parents dearly loved me and worked very hard to do what they could. I didn't want to be a burden, even at five. (Years later God would bring the joyful, find-humor-in-anything David Grant into my life to help "fix" my seriousness!)

Reading, learning, music, art, and storms were my favorite things. I'd take my rocking chair out under a weeping willow tree in our front yard whenever I heard thunder. (Looking back, I can't believe Mom let me do that!) Holding my umbrella over my head, I'd sit, watch, and feel the power of the storm moving in. The thunder sounded like God was moving His furniture around upstairs, and all was well. To this day, storms intrigue me and remind me that the God we serve is even greater than and above the storm.

Church was a vital part of our family's life every week. Pentecostal churches in the Potomac District in the 1950s were loud, emotional, and, for some of us children, exhausting. Some things were predictable, but other things were impossible to predict.

Blue-collar workers from our small mill town would show up in church, struggling with alcohol and all the heartbreak that comes with it. Others were military service members from nearby Fort Meade, the National Security Agency, and other governmental agencies surrounding the town of Savage. We were midway between Washington, DC, and Baltimore, and folks in the congregation couldn't have been more different from each other. But no matter what their socioeconomic status may have been, when the Spirit of God began to move as people worshipped and cried out to Him together, life-changing, miraculous things happened: People were healed. Others were filled with the Holy Spirit and spoke in tongues. The gifts of the Spirit were at work. Despite all my natural reserve and preference for quiet and order, the power and presence of God was undeniable.

It was not easy to be a reflective, reserved child in a Pentecostal church during those days. And things happened that, even as an eight-year-old, I was sure God had absolutely nothing to do with. One Sunday morning, shoes went flying across the front of the church during worship service because someone "got blessed." There were frequent spontaneous outbursts of joyful shouts, and certain saints often would take off and run around the church. I was petrified by those things, and when they happened, I would get closer to Mom. But my heart kept saying, "God, I want You. But I really don't want anything that isn't You."

By the time I reached my teens, I had begun to understand the New Testament exhortation for us to discern what is of God and what is not. Some of the things that happen when the Spirit of the Lord is poured out and people experience His presence, especially for the first time, are very human reactions to the supernatural revelation of God, His power, and His love. It can be overwhelming. Some of us grow quieter in awe. And some of us get louder, shout with joy, or dance. I had to learn that God is OK with different expressions of worship from people who have hearts that are hungry for Him.

Over time, it became apparent that I wasn't as smart as I thought I was. There was a man who got saved in our church and delivered from a very dark life. He had little education, but he had been forgiven much, and he loved much. When there was a move of the Holy Spirit in the service, he would frequently begin to pray in tongues. It always sounded the same and, to my young ears, nonsensical. So I concluded, "That can't be God."

Years later on one of my first ministry trips across the Pacific with my husband, we were going from one small Micronesian island to another. On each island some locals would deplane, and others would board for the next jaunt. At one point as we were taking off for the next short flight, I gasped: Two men sitting behind me conversing in a local island language were speaking the very same words that man in my home church half a world away had spoken twenty years earlier under the power of the Holy Spirit.

From that moment, I determined to be slower to judge and more ready to respect God when He's at work among those who fervently seek Him.

One Sunday morning when I was seven, a well-known evangelist and teacher named Carl Brumback came to my home church. After he preached, he invited people to make a decision to follow Jesus. Somehow, I knew Jesus was personally asking me to follow

7

Him, and I knew I needed Him to be the Lord of my life. All alone on the pew as others stood at the altar, I made the decision that would change the direction of my life and eternity: to give my life to Jesus and follow Him.

My experience that morning was quiet but deeply profound. When my parents returned to their seats, I was sure they would see a visible difference and ask me what had happened. They didn't, so I told them! That reality of "Beth following Jesus" is the truth that has defined my life to this day. People, seasons, ministry assignments, and positions come and go, but following Jesus remains the bedrock and defining identity of my life.

A need for quiet and time to reflect and pray became integral to my faith and learning to walk with God. I had lots of questions that didn't seem to be welcome at Bethel Assembly in the 1950s and '60s. But the more I grew in faith and pressed into God and His Word, the more He reassured me. He was not threatened by my sincere, searching questions. (I loved the Psalmist David! He asked great questions.) I learned we can be honest with God, and He will guide us. "Lord, I really don't understand," I would say. "But I choose to trust You."

My dad's love of music and worship was something we shared. It increasingly became a way for me to express my love and heart for God. Many nights, I went to sleep with Dad playing his guitar along with recordings of the legendary guitarist Chet Atkins. When I became church pianist and organist at fifteen, it was a joy to join my dad in countless hours of worship and altar services. Little steps in learning to be Spirit sensitive and Spirit led grew out of accompanying him those many hours a week of worship and intercession. When I didn't have words, my hands at the piano could express my worship and my heart, seeking God.

One of the greatest gifts my mom ever gave me was ensuring there was money for piano lessons. I loved classical music. When I was in middle and high school, lessons provided a way for me

A Tender, Feisty Faith

to connect with a world outside church as a choral accompanist. And my dad kept it all in balance by taking me with him to Black churches and camp meetings in Baltimore. He loved the music, and so did I.

At a Potomac Youth Camp when I was fourteen years old, I experienced the baptism of the Holy Spirit. Why did it take so long? It took time to find a way to create a quiet place with God in the middle of the intensity and volume of the prayer meetings! In those days a quiet teenager in a Pentecostal youth camp was a magnet for praying ladies that shouted to God and spit all over you in the process! I have laughingly said that God filled me with His Spirit in spite of it all. And I am so grateful He did.

Many years later my doctoral adviser and friend, Judy Lingenfelter, PhD, from Biola University, was our personal guest at an Assemblies of God (AG) National Conference for Women in Ministry. With one thousand women of the Spirit in one place, the firebrand Reverend Martha Tennison preached, and women were slain in the Spirit on the floor at Judy's feet during the prayer service. I was leading the service at the time and couldn't afford to be distracted from what God was saying to watch what was going on at the altar. But Judy was there, and while the demonstrations were new to her, I trusted her to honestly ask me questions about them later. Her decades of experience as a cross-cultural educator working in different cultures all over the world more than prepared her for respectfully going into diverse religious settings with an open mind and heart.

So when we finally got back home at midnight, she was chuckling as she said, "Beth, I know you. You're reserved and quiet. How do you do this? *Being Pentecostal must be exhausting!*" I laughed out loud; I loved her for asking. And then I told her a secret: There's an overlooked advantage to being people of the Spirit. Sometimes so much is going on in God's powerful presence that people are not paying much attention to the quiet ones among them. All that holy distraction gives us plenty of room to create a personal, quiet, Spirit-soaked place with God. And I guess that's what I'd been doing for a very long time.

A telling of my spiritual journey would not be complete without informing you about the significant influence Ms. Williams had on me growing up. Ms. Williams was really the adoptive grandmother in my life who was most present; she was involved in both my dad's and my mom's spiritual journeys too. She was born into a hardworking family in Charlottesville, Virginia, in very hard times, so she grew up spending more time working in the fields than going to school; in fact, she had only a second-grade education. Eventually, Ms. Williams married and had children—and then her husband died. She ended up in our community and became a part of Bethel Church.

Ms. Williams was in my life from the time I was born. She had become a spiritual mother to both my mom and my dad when they were still single, and she provided boarding for my dad before they married. So when I was born, and later when my brother was, Ms. Williams shared many meals with us, made many grocery runs, celebrated many birthday dinners, and was the one who had enough courage to ride with me when I was learning to drive.

Ms. Williams was a spiritual force for God. She was a woman of prayer, intercession, and the Word like no one else I knew. Whether she was walking into a person's home or the house of God, she brought God's presence and a sense of spiritual authority with her.

That's because, from her easy chair with a quilt in the corner of her small living room, she consumed God's Word daily and stormed heaven until God's glory filled the place. How did I

A Tender, Feisty Faith

know? When I would go by her house after school as a teenager, she would still be in that chair, and God's presence would be heavy. Then when I got old enough to date, it seemed like her eyes could look into my soul and bring conviction (not that anything was happening that needed conviction)! It was a look that said, "Don't be messin' around, girl! God's hand is on your life." Oh, Ms. Williams loved me dearly. But she was discerning, protective, and jealous over what she saw God doing in my life. I knew I needed to stay as close to God as I could because her eyes could always see exactly where I was.

When our church needed an adult Sunday school teacher, they called Ms. Williams. People would bring their backslid relatives to hear this widow with a second-grade education teach. Actually, the word *teach* doesn't quite get it; Ms. Williams had prayed so much over that class that when she taught, God's anointing on her was palpable. And in those moments in her Sunday school class, anything could happen. Prodigals who had lost their way would come back to Jesus and repent with tears. People smugly going about their business would be convicted of sin in their lives.

As a young girl I would slip out of my own class early to go to the back door of the sanctuary and peek in. I knew that when Ms. Williams was teaching and anointed, God would be in the place. I didn't want to miss those moments. The fire of God burned powerfully on His daughter.

Ms. Williams' presence in my life was one of the main reasons I never thought of the call and anointing of God as something only men received. I grew up watching a woman many would consider to be a pauper carry herself with the bearing of a queen because of the spiritual mantle that had been bestowed upon her. Grown men, whether blue-collar workers or military, were deeply moved as Ms. Williams shared God's Word.

And in my young heart, I knew I wanted to be that kind of woman of God.

LEFT: My parents, Hollis and Eleanor Oakes, were married on October 20, 1948, at Bethel Assembly of God in Savage, Maryland.

RIGHT: My second-grade school photo

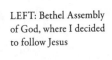

LEFT: Bethel Assembly of God, where I decided to follow Jesus

This is my little brother, Tim, and his daughter, Amy. He always had a big heart, was everybody's friend, and was a great guitarist like our dad.

I always loved being with my dad wherever we were in the world. When we were based in Belgium, he fit right in.

Chapter 2

An Unfolding Call

B Y MY MID-TEENS I had a growing sense that God's hand was on my life for ministry. There was no specific call to preach, to pastor, or to do missions. God was simply asking me to be available to Him—whenever, wherever, and however He would choose. In simple faith with no idea of what that would look like, everything in me said, "Yes, Lord."

There was a practical side to this yes. In a small Pentecostal church in the 1950s and '60s, the only professional minister was the pastor. So everything else that needed to be done in ministry and church life was done by church members who volunteered. We did it all at some point—gifted or not. But it provided me, along with others, a wealth of experience with church chores, with helping different kinds of ministry, and with people.

A new pastor named Ervin Mason was elected at Bethel when I was fifteen. I remember being one of a few teenagers who showed up the day he and his family arrived to help them move into the church apartment. One day, after being there a few months, he said to me, "Beth, God's hand is on your life." I was taken aback, amazed that what I had sensed privately and told no one, Brother Mason confirmed. The power of simple, unadorned prophetic words over a teenager's life can never be overestimated.

Soon after that the voting members of the church elected me as the youth leader. Now, the role of the youth leader at that time was to plan and convene weekly youth meetings, plus occasional social events for teenagers, and usually to speak at their first

An Unfolding Call

service on Sundays. Note the pastor, elders, and supporting parents all came to those services as well to make sure things stayed on track—and *youth* went up to age thirty-five!

I went to prayer in a panic. And the more I prayed, the more strongly God laid a challenging passage from Galatians 3 on my heart. The heart of it is verse 3: "Are you so foolish? After beginning with the Spirit, are you now trying to attain your goal by human effort?" (paraphrased).

Now, our church was more than a bit legalistic, and the youth who didn't even know that word felt it. Plus, I was only fifteen. This was my first responsibility with a God-given platform, and half of the group was adults and elders. "Are You sure, God?" I had no desire for public speaking beyond that service. But I certainly didn't want it to go badly.

That was the first time I spoke in public I remember vividly, trusting that *what I sensed God was saying to me was what He was surely saying.* I began that night with trepidation. But as I spoke each word, the sense of God's presence, power, and anointing grew stronger. The words flowed with His anointing. Genuine conviction of sin that can come only from the Spirit was heavy in that youth service. And by the end all of us— both old and young—were weeping and repenting as we went into prayer. It was a pivotal personal moment with God. As a teenage girl I was so humbled to realize that He could and would lead me if I sought Him with all my heart. He could anoint and speak through me if I would trust Him and obey His voice.

I didn't know it at the time, but that youth service began my journey of learning how God would tend to use me over the years. It wasn't that He could not or would not work through me in different ways at various times. But as one walks and ministers with friends, one begins to see specific spiritual gifts as God works in and through us. Recurrent biblical themes mark

15

our lives and ministries. From that point forward the words God burned into my soul would often be challenging ones on behalf of His truth, His justice, and His life-changing compassion. I had no idea at the time, but as I kept saying yes, God's specific ways and work for me became clearer. I grew to be at peace with the person He uniquely created me to be. There was no mold—only following and active submission to the master potter shaping my life and service, one step at a time.

God's promises to a young man named Jeremiah, who later became a prophet, spoke deeply to me through the Word as a teenager, and their meanings emerged more over the ensuing decades:

> "Before I formed you in the womb I knew you, before you were born I set you apart; I appointed you as a prophet to the nations."
>
> "Alas, Sovereign LORD," I said, "I do not know how to speak; I am too young."
>
> But the LORD said to me, "Do not say, 'I am too young.' You must go to everyone I send you to and say whatever I command you. Do not be afraid of them, for I am with you and will rescue you," declares the LORD.
>
> Then the LORD reached out his hand and touched my mouth and said to me, "I have put my words in your mouth."
>
> —JEREMIAH 1:5–9

By the time I was ready to graduate from high school, several things had become apparent.

First, I didn't have enough party in me to be the best youth leader. If you want prayer, call Beth. If you want to party, find

An Unfolding Call

somebody else. (That is still true to this day!) That was a baton to pass.

Second, my heart and confidence for ministry were growing, but I still had no specific direction. As my family and I prayed, God led me to apply for Towson State College and major in education instead of going to Bible college. That was unheard of in my home church. "Why would a Christian girl called to ministry go to a secular university?" people said. There was a not-so-subtle concern that if you wanted your children to stay in the faith, they needed to enroll in a Christian school.

In the late 1960s Towson State College in Baltimore was known as a solid school for teacher education. Since I had no clear, specific ministry calling to plan toward at that point and they offered me a full scholarship, and since I loved teaching and learning, Towson seemed like a good next step. God gave me peace about the decision, and my parents were supportive. I was seventeen.

I stepped onto campus into a student body of approximately ten thousand. The freshman year began with an infamous week of initiation when you showed up on the front lawn and did as an upperclassman told you. On the first afternoon, I was called out as one of eight freshmen girls to become a cheerleader, to do choreography, and to shout, "Shake your moneymaker!" over and over again until we reached the end of the field and a waiting crowd. I'd been raised to do whatever you have to do with enthusiasm. It was only when I literally got to the end of the field and we stopped moving that I realized what I was saying. What a way to start being a witness!

This was the Vietnam War era, and Towson State College became a hot spot for anti-war protests, flag burning, and the liberal group Students for a Democratic Society (SDS). On the commons there were candlelight vigils, flag burnings, and love-ins. The pacifist then-Father Philip Berrigan, who was

17

famously protesting the Vietnam War, spent time in a jail not far from my dorm.

In that era American youth were angry and disillusioned; they protested the Vietnam War and sparked the Sexual Revolution. And I was far from the world of my conservative Christian upbringing and Pentecostal church in every way but mileage.

But as challenging as it was, I knew God had led me there. As time went on, I began to see why. After living in a protective home of faith and devotion to Jesus, my "home" was now a dormitory where marijuana grew freely and classmates were coming in at all hours drunk and ghastly sick. I watched, unable to help, as they made decisions that would lead to heartache and contribute to their own loss of value and almost certain exploitation as women.

And I had a growing, humbling realization: With just one decision Beth could be headed down a similar road. I was not inherently better or more righteous than they were. By God's grace my parents had given me an opportunity to meet Jesus at an early age in a home where faith grew deep and strong. For most students around me there had been little to no such opportunity.

My first roommate was a friend from high school who soon learned her mother was dying of cancer. In her devastation I prayed for her and tried to comfort her. But a senior female student offered her more than I could: a more intimate relationship born out of grief and loss.

The second year, my roommate was a beautiful young woman from Tehran, Iran, named Scheherazade. Her family was wealthy, highly educated, and followed the Bahá'í religion. We soon learned that we had shared values: studies, excellence, modesty, and faith. Each night, I had my devotional time from my Bible, and she had hers from her Most Holy Book. We had ongoing

An Unfolding Call

conversations about faith. Her family was relieved she had found an American roommate who was a devoted person of faith.

And over the months, my heart broke—not for a theological concept called "the lost" but for young women who surrounded me every day. Each had a name and her own story, and I felt God's love for them. He sent Jesus for them, too. If His Word was true, God the Father was reaching for them. A determination grew in me to be available to love and reach for broken young women who had lost their way.

Do We Believe?

In a secular university one expects to find secular classes, content, curriculum, and worldviews. But God used my English literature course in a way I'll never forget. The professor was one of the most scathing, sarcastic, profane people I'd met in my life.

One day as we were studying *Paradise Lost* by John Milton— the story of Adam and Eve in the Garden of Eden and their fall from grace—the professor suddenly stopped mid-lecture, looked up from her notes, and said with sarcasm, "By the way, there are some people in the world who actually believe this is true." She hesitated, looked at the class of seventy-five students, and said, "There wouldn't happen to be anyone here who believes that, would there?"

An intimidating silence followed. And I thought, "If I do, I do." So, silently but with a smile, I raised my hand.

My professor was visibly taken aback as she looked condescendingly at me. But before she could say a word, ever so quietly—to her surprise and mine—fourteen other students began to slowly raise their hands too, one by one. Class was suddenly over, but the lesson wasn't.

On that day at the age of eighteen I decided I would own my faith no matter where God took me. I grew stronger. If I believed in Jesus and His Word, I needed to graciously and firmly own my belief, especially in a world that does not believe. I realized God knows where others are too—those who are timidly looking for someone to believe with, someone they can identify with and come closer to Jesus with.

Those two years at Towson were defining ones for God's call on my life. Out of ten thousand students an attempt to start a campus ministry yielded twelve who would identify as evangelicals, and that included several from nearby Johns Hopkins University. In that environment, both on and off campus, Presbyterians were viewed as far out, on the far edge. Pentecostals weren't even on the radar. It was lonely. But I learned to be part of a small minority of Jesus followers—small in number, but strong in faith in God. He was the God who sent His Son not to condemn the lost but that the lost through Him may be saved.

Importantly, in a secular university full of skepticism and non-Christian worldviews, I had opportunities to grapple with human knowledge in light of God's truth. There were times I could not understand or explain God or His ways intellectually. But I could never question His existence. I had personally experienced His power, presence, and miracles for seventeen years in a modest Pentecostal church. For me God's existence was undeniable, axiomatic. And when you think about it, any God an eighteen-year-old could get her mind around intellectually couldn't be a very big God after all, could He?

At that turning point in my life my parents wordlessly communicated a truth to me that would serve me well years later with my own two daughters: Mom and Dad were not afraid I would lose my faith by being in an environment where it would be challenged. Their willingness to bless me to go where I felt God was leading expressed their faith in the God to whom they had dedicated me as a baby. But it also communicated that they

An Unfolding Call

believed my experience with Him was real and strong. Their trust inspired my trust.

If they had been afraid, it would have made me wonder if God indeed was the only true God, trustworthy beyond all other gods. Did we serve Him solely because Christianity was the only religion we'd known? Towson gave me new reasons to know that God indeed is real, that He is good, and that He is with those who put their faith and trust in Him! And He is more compassionate for the lost and the broken in our world than we are.

Ms. Williams, an adoptive grandmother who inspired me as a child and teenager, was a powerful woman of God's Word, an intercessor, and an anointed teacher.

A very serious seventeen-year-old me in 1967 when I was a senior at Howard High School in Ellicott City, Maryland

Chapter 3

No Turning Back

THE ASSEMBLIES OF God began to offer international mission trips for teenagers during my freshman year of college, and I was intrigued by the possibilities. Along with a small group of other teenagers, I was accepted to be part of an outreach team in the mountains of central Jamaica.

This was not your tourist Jamaica. A month of daily outreach and nightly evangelistic meetings in local communities brought us face-to-face with women and children living in abject physical poverty. Many were immersed in the dark, demonic power of voodoo and the occult. That was a time of leaning in to God's heart for hurting people in another culture.

On those steep mountain paths our team learned to walk in God's power and anointing in order to minister to the people around us. It was painfully apparent to a group of teens on a cross-cultural mission that if anyone was going to be saved, healed, or delivered from Satan's bondage, it would be done by God at work through His Spirit as only He can do. In a time of personal devotions during that trip I sensed God telling me, "Beth, this will be your future. Ministry will not be *part* of your life; this will *be* your life." Amazingly, that month had been the most challenging and fulfilling month I'd ever experienced up to that point.

God's clear direction in Jamaica pointing me to vocational ministry led me to transfer from Towson to Central Bible

College (CBC) in Springfield, Missouri, for ministerial training my junior year. But in going there, I found more than I expected.

My first week on campus, I met a wonderfully gifted young man from Toledo, Ohio, named Brian Shaffer. He was outgoing, had a wonderful sense of humor, was a total people person, and loved music ministry as I did. Brian was gifted in so many things I was not. It was a joy to begin music ministry together while we were still in school through leading a traveling ministry ensemble called Newborn Singers for two years. Some of those team members are friends and ministry colleagues to this day. A week after my graduation, Brian and I were married.

Brian, however, still had two years to go. During that time, I had the opportunity to work in the school's music department as a vocal accompanist on the piano for Professor Mable Thompson's students. Ms. Thompson was a gifted and disciplined vocalist in her sixties, and she had little patience for students who were undisciplined. They had to step up to her bar of hard work and excellence, or they tended to burst into tears (girls) or to disappear from lessons (boys). There was a rigor and strength to Ms. Thompson personally and to the expectations she had for her accompanists as well. You were not there to be a wimpy background musician to the vocalist. She meant it to be an equal collaboration of strengths flowing together between the vocalist and accompanist.

Ms. Thompson, the choirmaster for Christ Episcopal Church, was tucked into a small studio in the back of Central Bible College. She and her husband were both professionally connected to Drury University and supporters of the arts. Ms. Thompson was highly respected in the city as a professional musician—and she wore makeup, which none of the women in my Potomac District denomination were allowed to do. Looking back, it is amazing to me that she was invited to teach voice to generations of Assemblies of God young people called to ministry.

24

No Turning Back

Ms. Thompson pushed me as an accompanist, and I grew in my skills with confidence and courage. But she also mentored me during those couple of years by her approach to life and ministry. Ms. Thompson taught me that when it's time to show up, you show up. You prepare beyond the level of what you believe you need to do, and when it's time to perform, you perform. Nerves do not stop you. They are incidental to what you have already worked hard and practiced well to do. What you need to deliver is already in your voice. You're next on the recital program. Step up, stand tall, breathe deep, and do what you've prepared to do.

Ms. Thompson would put the fear of God in you. And though she worked hard to hide it, she loved her students and gave them everything she had in every lesson. On good days, bad days, and emotional days, she taught me to bring my hands to the keys with strength and skill—even when the song itself was quiet. Quietness is not a lack of strength. It is strength under control with skill.

To my knowledge Ms. Thompson was not Pentecostal. But she prepared hundreds of future Pentecostal ministers and missionaries with a staunch faith, and she instilled the discipline many of us, and our music, needed!

There was one other professor at CBC who left a mark on my life, even though I never had her for a class: Opal Reddin, DMin, who was known for her teaching and preaching. She was particularly respected and remembered for the powerful anointing of the Holy Spirit on her platform ministry. The fire of God burned on this woman's life, ministry, and writing. Male and female students alike made sure not to skip chapel when Sister Reddin was going to preach. Many of us women called to ministry—whether that included preaching or not—hoped to be like her one day.

25

LEADING WITH A WHISPER

When Brian graduated two years later, we accepted an assignment to be ministers of music and youth at a church in Wilmington, Delaware. Rev. Asa Martin, his family, and the people of First Assembly of God were so welcoming, and we embraced the ministry opportunities God provided during our time there. He was good.

But after a year, Brian and I both began to sense God was preparing us for change and transition. We prayed, talked, and wondered what His stirring could mean. Were we to resign and take another assignment? Passages of Scripture, particularly in Psalm 27, came alive as Brian and I prayed and sought God.

> The LORD is my light and my salvation—whom shall I fear? The LORD is the stronghold of my life—of whom shall I be afraid?
>
> When the wicked advance against me to devour me, it is my enemies and my foes who will stumble and fall. Though an army besiege me, my heart will not fear; though war break out against me, even then I will be confident.
>
> One thing I ask from the LORD, this only do I seek: that I may dwell in the house of the LORD all the days of my life, to gaze on the beauty of the LORD and to seek him in his temple. For in the day of trouble he will keep me safe in his dwelling; he will hide me in the shelter of his sacred tent and set me high upon a rock.
>
> Then my head will be exalted above the enemies who surround me; at his sacred tent I will sacrifice with shouts of joy; I will sing and make music to the LORD.
>
> Hear my voice when I call, LORD; be merciful to me and answer me. My heart says of you, "Seek his face!" Your face, LORD, I will seek....

No Turning Back

> I remain confident of this: I will see the goodness of
> the LORD in the land of the living. Wait for the LORD;
> be strong and take heart and wait for the LORD.
> —PSALM 27:1–8, 13–14

One day while Brian was at church, I was in our apartment praying, playing the piano, and singing one of my favorite songs: "I have decided to follow Jesus! No turning back, no turning back." As I started to get up from the piano bench, a voice I had come to know stopped me: "Beth, look at verse two. Can you sing that to Me with all your heart as well?"

Verse two of the familiar hymn says, "Though none go with me, still I will follow. No turning back. No turning back."

And in that moment in God's heavy presence, I knew He does nothing without purpose. Quietly, through tears and with resolve I started over and began to sing each word to Jesus: "Though none go with me, still I will follow. No turning back!"

God knew I preferred not to walk out His call alone. But yes— if necessary, I would follow Him all by myself.

Three weeks later a police officer came to our apartment door and told me there had been an accident and I needed to go with him. He took me to the local hospital, where I learned that Brian had died.

In that moment, the first thing that came to my mind was, "God, You are good. You knew what lay ahead for Brian and for me. You loved Brian so much that You drew him closer to Yourself. And You cared so much about me that You prepared me for this moment." I had never known more personally that God knew where I was and was holding me in His hands than I did in that moment of unthinkable loss.

In the days that followed Brian's death any future at all was unimaginable. If I had any moments when I asked, "Why, God?" they would have been asking why Brian was gone and I remained.

LEADING WITH A WHISPER

He was so gifted and, at twenty-five years of age, had so much potential to live out his life and ministry for God. I had been completely at peace being a supportive, side-by-side, less public partner in ministry. I couldn't imagine the next day, let alone the next week, of my life without him.

Then on the day of Brian's memorial service a word from God came to me from a most unexpected source.

Brian's parents and mine were sitting with me after his service was over at the dining table in the small apartment I had shared with Brian. Suddenly, Brian's father—the very quiet Sam Shaffer—looked at me through the tears that were filling his eyes and flowing down his cheeks. "Beth," he said sincerely, "I can't wait to see what God has planned for your life."

I was stunned. I had no words. The most important prophetic words spoken over my life during the time after Brian's death came from his heartbroken father in the middle of his own loss. What a priceless, unselfish gift of hope.

The people of First Assembly Wilmington proved to be such a gracious and caring family in the year after Brian's death. Pastor Asa Martin and the rest of the church leadership invited me to remain on pastoral staff as the minister of music and education, as well as director of their kindergarten and preschool. The ability to give myself fully to people and ministries I loved was a gracious gift—and to walk with those who also were grieving Brian's death was comforting. The children, especially in the church preschool where I worked part-time, were particularly comforting.

"Ms. Beth, where is Mr. Brian?" they would ask.

"He's in heaven now with Jesus," I would tell them.

And they'd simply respond, "Oh, OK."

In those moments, I would find myself thinking, "Yes, he *is* OK now."

Grief is real, even for those of us who have a precious hope of

No Turning Back

heaven. But when we have loved well, we have reason to grieve well too. And sharing that journey of grieving with church family as part of the community of faith was a God-ordained strength and gift I had never experienced before. During that season people would say, "Beth, you are so strong." My reply then and to this day is, "No, I'm not strong. I'm desperate for God. And I know it." His strength indeed is made perfect in our weakness.

And God was still good—even when I didn't understand (and still don't understand to this day). But His very presence was with me in powerful and practical ways in my aloneness.

The worst time of day is nightfall, when all the work and busyness cease, and you suddenly realize how empty your apartment is. When you have been married, suddenly the gaping emptiness beside you in your bed is so cold you cannot sleep. I began to pray a specific prayer as part of my bedtime routine: "Father, I choose to trust You even though I do not understand. You have promised to be all I need. Would You please fill this cold, empty room with the warmth of Your tangible presence? Come, Lord. Cover me with the warmth of Your peace, and give rest for my mind, body, and spirit. I trust You. In Jesus' name I pray, amen."

As a young widow I learned to pray very practical and honest prayers. And day by day, night by night, God met me in the ways and places I needed Him most. I would not let Him go. He proved Himself to be a close and loving Father with whom I could entrust my very life.

No. There would be no turning back.

Chapter 4

God's Gift of David

SIX WEEKS BEFORE Brian died, we accompanied our church youth group to a camp in Pennsylvania. For two weeks we served with the camp worship team and counselors, ministering to the teenagers.

The speaker at the youth camp was a dynamic missionary-evangelist from western Florida named David Grant. The first night he preached, I had a strong physical reaction: He was the loudest preacher I'd ever heard in my life! I tried to find an outline for (or impose one on) his sermons for two weeks and never found one. But night after night, teenagers and staff alike were riveted by the messages of this passionate, funny, and powerfully anointed young man of God. David Grant had people laughing one moment and crying the next. After several nights, I realized that no one listening to him, young or old, would leave with a sermon outline. Instead, all were deeply impacted by hearing God the Father's broken heart for a broken world, and especially His heart for the land of India. David Grant was not like any missionary I had ever heard before.

Brian and I became friends with David during those two weeks. Both of them were energetic leaders, funny, and charismatic, and they thoroughly enjoyed life and people. By the end of the camp, Brian had invited David to visit us in Wilmington whenever he was in the area.

Shortly after the camp, David returned to India for ministry. But when he returned to the US several months later, he heard

God's Gift of David

about Brian's death from some of our mutual friends and called this young widow to share his condolences and see how she was doing.

For almost a year David called from wherever he was in the world—day or night because of time differences—to see how I was. Inevitably, he had a way of making me laugh. He could find humor in almost anything.

Throughout the months, Brian's parents, Sam and Jeannette Shaffer, and I kept in close touch. About ten months after Brian's death they invited me to join them for their annual two-week camping trip across Colorado. Driving from Toledo, Ohio, and back through beautiful mountain passes and parks provided precious time to share together. During that time, Sam and Jeannette brought up my future. They lovingly let me know that at twenty-five years of age I was much too young to not begin to have a social life again and remarry. Once more, Sam and now Jeannette stunned me with their sensitivity and faith for my future. Little did they or anyone else know I was receiving random phone calls and funny cards from a missionary-evangelist. I was uncertain about what to do with that. But Sam and Jeannette opened that door.

After a year of friendly phone calls and receiving notes scrawled on stationery and toilet paper from hotels around the world, David called and invited me to lunch. He said he was coming through the Philadelphia airport on his way back to India. (I only discovered much later that he was actually flying out of Los Angeles for India that night.) But I thought lunch sounded safe. When an old boyfriend contacted me a few months before, David was the one I shared my feelings of discomfort with. That contact had been inappropriate and very awkward. David knew I was not ready to think about any other future relationship after Brian's death.

I was wrong about it being safe. We met at a coffee shop

31

LEADING WITH A WHISPER

not far from the church, and David got right to the point. "I've prayed about this," he said. "I love you, and I believe I'm going to marry you. But you're under no pressure."

I remember thinking, "This is either the most presumptuous man I've ever met—or he has the most faith."

The only polite words I could find were, "You're entitled to your opinion."

David knew I had no interest in marrying again, but he assured me he would wait until he returned from India *two months later* for my answer! This was a man in a hurry, and I couldn't understand why. (Later I would find out that after learning someone from my past had already contacted me wanting to reopen a relationship, David felt he needed to act quickly and decisively.)

Like most do when they don't know what to say, I said, "I'll pray about it."

David returned to India, and I was desperate to hear from God. I had not dated this man, and my heart, mind, and spirit were all in turmoil. We were very different in temperaments, in personalities, and in our family cultures, and it was scary. To me David seemed impetuous, ambitious, and brash, while I was a planner, cautious; I took time to think and pray things through. Also, as a young married woman I watched David Grant leave multiple young women hopeful at those youth camps, so I wasn't sure I could trust his intentions.

So along with "I'll pray about it," I added, "You are a game player. And at this point in my life I don't need games. So if you want games, you need to look elsewhere."

I was taken aback by his immediate reply. "Yes, I have been a game player, and I'm good at it. But this is different. When you play games, you never lay all your cards on the table. But for the first time in my life I'm laying all my cards down. I've already contacted the young woman I've been seeing and told her I've

32

God's Gift of David

met the woman I'm going to marry. So she won't be seeing me again." And I thought, "This may be more serious than I realized."

One thing had come out of months of random phone calls. I already knew a lot about David Grant. Our faith, a passion to fulfill God's call with courage, and our home church cultures in Maryland and western Florida couldn't have been more alike. As children we both sang, "I'll go where You want me to go, dear Lord; I'll be what You want me to be." And without saying it I knew that for both of us there would be no turning back from giving our lives to God.

During those months of desperately seeking God's will in private while remaining silent with this persuasive man, something began to happen in my time with God. A powerful image from Genesis began to drive my prayer. In it the Holy Spirit hovered over a chaotic precreation Earth where there was no form, order, or beauty. And in that process God created form, order, and beauty.

"Please, God, hover in the same way by Your Spirit over my chaotic heart, mind, and spirit," I would pray. "Please bring order, clarity, direction, and peace!"

Amazingly, over the weeks as I sat quietly in God's presence, His reassuring direction became clear. What was humanly unknown became supernaturally known: David Grant indeed was a gift from God to me for life. And I was a gift from God to him.

But I also knew that many (that's David's word!) women might have married him for the promising, successful, good days of favor he was enjoying in missions and our movement. But God quietly reminded me that He brought me into David's life to walk with him through the days to come that would not be so promising as well. There would be difficult days when leaders and followers would not be so enthusiastic and supportive.

I was already familiar with loss. I chose to marry David for all the great days of victory ahead that God would give us in faith. And I chose to marry him in order to be by his side on the most difficult days of our life to come. I had learned to be at peace in a storm.

Five months later on December 22, 1976, David Grant and Beth Shaffer were married before four hundred dear family members and friends at First Assembly of God in Wilmington, Delaware.

And Sam and Jeannette Shaffer were thrilled and celebrated with us. They quickly grew to admire and love David. Jeannette in particular, who had a delightful, infectious sense of humor, loved to laugh at his stories.

~~~~~

With one *I do* the theme song of my life went from Handel's *Messiah* to Willie Nelson's "On the Road Again," from English muffins to southern biscuits.

Even before we left the church at midnight after our wedding, instead of seeing us off on our two-day honeymoon, two of David's brothers approached our car and started to kidnap me. They announced to him, "You've waited thirty years; you can wait one more night!" And to everyone's shock—including his own—David Grant, the preacher in the family, punched his big brother in the face.

His stunned brothers let me go, and David and I drove off to begin our very exciting new life together.

That was the beginning of learning so much from my new, big southern family. My first dinner with the Grants consisted of fourteen people who were there to meet and welcome me, all talking loudly at the same time. David's sweet mom noticed the overwhelmed look on my face and said, "Honey, you're trying to listen, aren't you? Nobody listens around here!"

God's Gift of David

Yes, I do love to listen, and I married a man who loves to be listened to. Fortunately for me he's a captivating, motivating, and entertaining communicator. In addition to our marriage vows David told me he couldn't promise me any of the worldly things by which some people measure success—but I would never die of boredom.

That man has kept his word.

David and I departed for India together a week after our wedding, and the warm welcome we received in each city we visited was overwhelming. David had already been ministering there for nine years when we met; as a result he had a wealth of friends and leaders all over the nation who viewed him as a spiritual son or brother. Only upon arrival did I hear that David had promised them he would be coming back in January 1977 with a wife.

That was before I even agreed to marry him.

To this day I am overcome by deep emotions when I remember the grace and kindness with which my new Indian friends received me. They loved David Grant, and they would love me. I had never experienced such a gracious hospitality and welcome in my life.

But there was another side of traditional Indian culture, which David and I were both unaware of. In our first open-air public meeting together, David was to preach to about ten thousand people. He was on the platform to minister, and I was seated on the front row of the women's side of the grounds with other female leaders who were friends. Hundreds of local women and their children surrounded me.

When David was introduced, the crowd welcomed him with great excitement. Then he introduced his new wife, Beth, who previously had been a widow—and immediately, the crowd went

LEADING WITH A WHISPER

silent. We had expected celebration. But instead, people began to talk out loud among themselves in hushed tones of shocked disbelief. "David Grant married a widow?"

Something was wrong. It took the national leader to bring the crowd back to order before David could preach.

After the service the leader, David's friend Rev. Y. Jeyaraj, told him privately, "Brother Grant, it would be better if you never mentioned that Beth was a widow again. In our culture no one would ever marry a widow. She is considered a curse, and she would even bear some responsibility for her husband's death in our traditional culture. No Indian man would marry a widow."

He then added, "We love you, and we will love Beth. But it's best to never mention it again."

In that moment I realized what the leader was saying, even if David did not: In Indian culture I was considered damaged goods. My life and ministry journey really were starting over.

The next morning David was scheduled to preach at a large pastors' meeting. If I had wondered before whether I married a courageous man, I would wonder no more after that.

David went to the podium and with spiritual authority began to read from the Old Testament:

> Sing to God, sing in praise of his name, extol him who rides on the clouds; rejoice before him—his name is the LORD. A father to the fatherless, *a defender of widows*, is God in his holy dwelling.
> —PSALM 68:4–5, EMPHASIS ADDED

> Learn to do right; seek justice. Defend the oppressed. Take up the cause of the fatherless; *plead the case of the widow*.
> —ISAIAH 1:17, EMPHASIS ADDED

God's Gift of David

From scripture to scripture, with God's very own words, David proclaimed God's heart and loving concern for widows. Mature men of God began to quietly weep as the Holy Spirit brought conviction for how they had viewed and treated widows in their churches. Several stood and repented with tears, asking God to forgive them for treating widows and orphans the same way their non-Christian culture and other religions did instead of hearing and obeying God's Word.

And just that quickly into my journey with David, God had given me a humbling way of identifying with Indian women that I did not anticipate. My very life story spoke to the truths that there is new life, hope, and healing and that Jesus' redemptive purposes are available for all women, even those whom culture and the church may write off as damaged goods. Part of the radical nature of the gospel is that God Himself has good plans for all daughters who determine to put their trust in Him.

The seed of a prophetic message for women was planted in my heart those first weeks in India. And through God's mysterious ways it would become a theme for His mission, proclaimed by David's life and mine for years to come. Out of my time of lament, God would birth a life-giving song in my soul for women across a great nation.

A STEEP AND WONDERFUL LEARNING CURVE

David and I married knowing the most important things about each other after hundreds of phone calls. But we didn't know each other in practical ways, as you do if you have had a dating relationship over time.

For example, David came from a Southern Pentecostal pioneer preacher's family that moved to a different state almost every year while he was growing up. His parents—Pastor Curtis Grant and

37

LEADING WITH A WHISPER

Bonnie Grant—made sure their parsonages were always open to guests, and David's grandmother Mawmaw's vegetables, biscuits, and sweet iced tea were always ready to welcome the world.

So David and his four siblings learned to share everything with everyone. They grew up having big hearts for people and holding material things lightly. The idea of individual ownership of anything was a bit foreign, and this applied not only to physical and financial possessions but also to time and space. As David would later write in his book, *Born to Give*, his parents successfully raised extraordinarily generous children who welcomed the world into their own homes, their spaces, and their lives. They were inspiring! They lived sacrificially.

But to someone raised in a small nuclear family in the Mid-Atlantic, whose father came from New England, whose mother was of good German stock, and whose parents both worked and lived on a schedule, David Grant's world was a bit overwhelming at first. There were two *p* words I didn't know were high priorities for me until I didn't have them: *privacy* and *peace*. The Grant family seemed to prioritize neither. In their world the question seemed to be, Why would anyone want privacy?

When the extended Grant family got together, it was always highly entertaining. There were fireworks between siblings, great humor, laugh-until-you-cry funny family stories, and recollections of God's miraculous deeds through Pastor Grant and Bonnie's ministry. Their home was always characterized by great faith in God, generosity, and colorful personalities. People in the community who struggled to find the narrow way and stay on it were always welcome at the Grants' humble parsonage. Grace lived there.

But peace? My mom, dad, baby brother, and I avoided conflict and tense topics. Our motto was, "Keep the peace. If it's not important, let it go." Mostly, my dad was a very peaceful, avoid-conflict-at-all-costs kind of man. But when he was upset,

God's Gift of David

he'd start whistling. If it really got bad, he would disappear for a while and take a walk. (But once, he did take my boyfriend by the collar and put him out the front door. It was dinnertime, and Dad was a meat and potatoes man; messing with his meal was not allowed!)

But at the Grants' if it got quiet in the family, one of David's brothers or his sister would intentionally bring up a sensitive topic to light a fire. They all relished a good fight! I learned to enjoy their dynamics and differences from my own family but also to disappear when I needed to.

Twenty years into our marriage David and I were doing an activity together that required us to identify our top five personal values in life. After all that time, my dear husband looked shocked when he saw I had listed *peace* as one of those five. In all seriousness he said, "Why would you choose *peace*?"

Yes, I know God arranged our marriage. But in the process of becoming one, David Grant rocked my peace. God knew I needed some spontaneity and joy to bring balance to all my seriousness. And He also knew that the fiery young evangelist going off in every direction at once "for the glory of God!" needed a peaceful heart and an ordered, quiet place to call home—wherever we might be in the world.

David and I were married on December 22, 1976, at First
Assembly of God in Wilmington, Delaware.

At our commissioning with the Assemblies of God World Missions in Springfield,
Missouri, in 1977, David's mentor and leader, legendary missionary Charles
Greenaway, prayed over him, and David's father, Pastor Curtis Grant, prayed over me.

Chapter 5

India Captured My Heart

OUR FIRST YEAR together in India brought great joys and some challenges.

The land and its cultures were full of beauty and diversity beyond what I could have imagined. Vibrant colors brought life and joy in the forms of flowers, birds, bustling markets, palaces, and women's saris. There was an amazing amount of life and laughter coming from children who lived in the most economically challenged areas. Rich expressions of family and community were seen everywhere in ways that were beyond my cultural, independent way of thinking at that time. Americans think of their history in terms of hundreds of years, but in India I found a land of wealth and growing technological innovation alongside ancient history and tradition that spanned *thousands* of years. My love of history, geography, cultures, and learning quickly kicked in with David's, who to my delight turned out to be an explorer from birth.

Little did I know that I had married an expert traveler and authority on the history and cultures of Southern Asia. In every city where we landed, David gave me history lessons and cultural insights as our taxi drivers drove like Jehu through twisted city streets. Over the years I would hear from appreciative Indian nationals throughout Southern Asia, Europe, and the United States, "This man knows our nation better than we do!" I was privileged to learn from the best, not just from the facts about those places but from the heart of a people too.

The cultural, economic, religious, and social issues of one of the world's largest nations have now become familiar and even iconic around the world through media. But when you immerse yourself among a people, there are more subtle treasures to be discovered that lead to admiration and joy. This is especially true of guests who want to learn a culture in order to understand and value it, because their passion is to know and love a people the same way Jesus loves them.

Several aspects of Indian culture and the family of God were particularly inspiring and challenging to me as a woman, a minister, and a member of the community of faith in those early days. Each contributed, in time, to who I would become as a wife, mother, minister, leader, and daughter of God.

1. Indian women in ministry informed my model of what it means to be a strong, courageous woman of God and influence. Before leaving the United States, it was customary for me as a female minister to enter a church, staff, or social meeting and interact with both men and women. But when I first started entering the homes of church leaders and colleagues in India, it was apparent that local female colleagues and wives gravitated to other women naturally. Before long I watched as women ended up visiting with women at social functions, and men with men. And frequently, if there was a kitchen, the women gravitated there to chat and be helpful to the rest of the group.

Coming from a more egalitarian culture in America, at first this seemed awkward, and I missed having the opportunity to have conversations with male leaders alongside my husband. But over time I began to realize strong women gravitating to other strong women in our faith community was an opportunity for iron to sharpen iron. First impressions of new cultures can be deceiving and hide strengths and competencies that look quite different from our own. These strong, wise women who did not call attention to themselves earned my growing respect as they

India Captured My Heart

discreetly handled complicated problems in families, churches, and communities while gathering in kitchens, with tea and biscuits, as they hosted countless guests together.

My Indian sisters in ministry had been raised in a more indirect, hierarchical culture that had very clearly defined female and male roles. But they knew intuitively how to use their God-given influence and gifts in less direct ways. (I don't think I had an indirect bone in my body at the time.) They kindly welcomed American colleagues and me into their homes, families, prayer meetings, and faith communities, despite my sometimes direct ways. And on my journey with them I found myself growing more in grace and courage, like them.

This direct New England, German, East Coast missionary was given the gift of walking closely with my diplomatic Indian sisters for forty-five years. Ministry leaders' wives in India navigate complex issues in a challenging world where daughters are viewed as less valuable than sons. They can move from the kitchen to the platform to mediating interpersonal conflicts and then head back to the kitchen from which they host the nations. Along with their husbands and colleagues they are passionately devoted to raising their families for the Lord, helping plant churches, building life-changing ministries, educating, and serving communities with the compassion of Jesus.

But that close walk with my Southern Asian friends also brought me uncomfortably face-to-face with some aspects of my own cultural hypocrisy. I remember hearing some of the women I was friends with back home complain because in their cultures or denominations they were being restricted to ministry for women and children. I think in my college years I may have shared some of that sentiment. Then when I found myself in a nation that is home to one-sixth of the world's population, and a majority of those 1.5 billion people are women and children with God-given potential, I had to ask myself a troubling question: "How can

43

LEADING WITH A WHISPER

ministry devoted to a majority of people across all the nations of the world possibly be viewed as a restriction?"

I began to admit, as I searched my heart, that ministry focused entirely on God's daughters can only be viewed as a negative if that view is shaped by my cultural sense of personal rights and dislike of any perceived restrictions. If we love the daughters of God and value them as He does—*and as much as we say we do and ask other people to*—ministry dedicated to them cannot be considered less than. The church globally has a God-given mission for women and girls to come to know Jesus along with men and boys and, beyond that, for them to be anointed with His Spirit's power so they can literally impact their cities, their nations, and the world! If they receive the gospel freely as their Father intended, and if they are discipled and filled with His Spirit, millions of women and daughters across the nations can become vibrant lights in darkened places. And like Deborah the prophetess in the Book of Judges, I believe some of them will become generals in the Lord's army! Many of them have done so already.

2. Indian believers challenged me to a whole new level of intercession and prayer. From the time David first took me to India, our days were spent with churches that were devoted to countless hours of fervent worship and prayer every week. The intensity of intercession, service after service, was spiritually formidable. Whether David and I were in small church plants or mature churches of thousands, people of God would cry out to Him en masse with loud voices. They stormed the gates of hell with a faith that seizes God's promises and prays in obedience in the power of the Spirit. When I stepped on the grounds or passed through doors of many places of worship and prayer, I would literally sense I had entered a holy place. God's presence filled the temple, and He Himself was moving.

Powerful all-night prayer meetings were common and ongoing

India Captured My Heart

in the calendars of churches in Southern Asia. One of those all-night prayer meetings in particular was unforgettable for me.

A great pastor friend was leading thousands of members of his congregation, hour after hour, in intercession for specific needs as the Spirit led him. As was common, the concert of prayer would crescendo like waves rising and falling in intercession and praise to a mighty God.

Suddenly, the leader began to pray a prophetic prayer with power that was worthy of the Old Testament prophets. The audacity and immensity of his prayer for his city and the subcontinent took my breath. This prayer was proclaimed over loudspeakers within the church but no doubt could also be heard for blocks around it. The voice of that mighty man of God was a cry shaking the gates of hell on behalf of his beloved nation.

It occurred to me that I had never prayed a prayer that big and courageous in my life. I was convicted by it. Why had I never prayed that way? It struck me that I had a cultural handicap that hindered me when I came to God in intercession. In my good, independent upbringing in New England I had been taught that it was impolite, even inappropriate, to ask anyone for something unless it was absolutely necessary. If you did ask, you were to ask conservatively and even apologetically.

Then on my faith journey I came to Scripture. God Himself invited His people to ask Him for things in prayer that are in accordance with His good will and purposes. Jesus instructed His disciples—commanded them!—to "ask, and it will be given to you" (Matt. 7:7, esv). In that Southern Asian prayer meeting it hit me that my cultural upbringing influenced how I heard Jesus' command to ask. He invited His disciples, including me, to pray in faith boldly and largely for the very things God Himself has ordained and promised. Apologetically asking and conservatively seeking God were pale substitutes for spiritually storming heaven!

That night, this young missionary, me, repented. "Father,

45

forgive me for praying small, pitiful prayers that are not worthy of You, mighty God and Creator of the heavens and earth! From this time, set me free to pray courageous, far-reaching prayers of faith that are born of Your Word and Spirit. Teach me to pray prayers that will take on the powers of darkness and take hold of all You have intended for Your kingdom's mission in our world! In the powerful name of Jesus I pray and believe, amen!"

Since that night, Beth Grant's prayers have never been quite the same.

3. Indian fathers and brothers in leadership discerned God's call on my life and, in time, opened doors for ministry. Southern Asian culture is inherently gracious, and the Christian communities hosting guests are no exception. So when ministers like my husband were traditionally invited to preach, their spouses were often asked to "bring greetings" before the sermon.

On our first trip together I looked to David. "What do I do?" I asked. "What do I say?"

He made it sound so simple. "Oh, just greet the people; say you're happy to be with them. And if you have a verse on your heart, you can share it. No problem." (I was thinking, "That's easy for you to say.") But I can follow instructions, so I did. Hundreds of times, on hundreds of new and different platforms, David Grant's quiet wife addressed hundreds of people, bringing greetings.

But something happened over time as I walked side by side with David and step by step with God. As I'd step up to bring greetings, God began to stir my heart for the hundreds to thousands of people sitting in front of me. I sensed the overwhelming greatness of His love for them. And since He is the God who still speaks, He began to drop scriptures and words into my heart—just a few encouraging words for people in that place and that moment in time. Gradually, God helped me

India Captured My Heart

listen more carefully to His still, small voice and lean in to those meaningful moments with faith.

Through years of such services and traditional cultural moments I learned to simply be discerning and available to the One we can trust. In the moments we may consider ceremonial and possibly insignificant, I experienced God at work. By His Spirit and with our obedience He can do deeply transformative things. Don't overlook the little moments, the small open doors, the ordinary spots on a service run sheet. They're only ordinary when we assume there's a temporary absence of the One who has the power to speak and minister to the people He loves. In God's economy moments matter.

Over the years, David and I watched God work in mysterious ways. Pastor friends continued to ask me to bring greetings before David preached. But a few would add with a whisper and a smile, "And Sister Beth, take all the time you want!"

MENTORS MATTER TOO

As David and I served together in Southern Asia, God used several great local leaders as mentors who spoke prophetically into my life and emerging ministry as well as into David's. At times when I was reluctant to step out in faith for cultural or personal reasons, they were friends who encouraged me to step up. One national leader began to invite me to preach for one of the multiple services where tens of thousands came weekly to meet God and receive prayer. But for several years I found good reasons to decline his gracious invitations.

Then one day, he said with his invitation, "Sister Beth, God speaks through you. We need to hear what He has to say. Don't hesitate to speak the words He gives you." He added, "I have you scheduled for one of tomorrow morning's services."

The pastor's words were the most gracious gut punch of

47

LEADING WITH A WHISPER

conviction I'd ever experienced. He was right. I quietly said yes and repented with tears that day because I realized I had been so concerned about being culturally sensitive that I prioritized being a woman and a wife over sharing the words God was clearly burning into my soul. The God who speaks births life-giving, prophetic words for moments, times, and places. He used this great, humble man of God and friend to speak spiritual truth into my life like a brother. A new season of ministry was being born.

The elderly, esteemed, wise general superintendent of India, Rev. Y. Jeyaraj, who led the first service where David introduced me as a widow, later became an encouraging spiritual father and advocate for my personal ministry. Whenever I was speaking somewhere in his vast nation, he would somehow surprisingly show up. These leaders in Southern Asia and their wives blessed David's life and ministry—and they deeply blessed mine too.

Over decades with our adoptive family, David and I have fought some fierce spiritual battles, celebrated miraculous victories, and experienced the always-sufficient grace of God!

LEFT: This was one of my first steps into public ministry in India.

RIGHT: Our family was at AG Mission, Kolkata, with Rev. Huldah Buntain at the memorial for her husband, Rev. Dr. Mark Buntain. The Buntains' passion for the people of their great city and their presentation of the whole gospel to the poor deeply inspired the ministry of compassion David and I led.

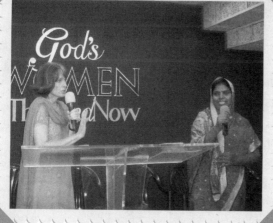

LEFT: We're ministering at the First National AG Women Ministers' Conference in India. The theme was, "God's Women: Then and Now."

Chapter 6

Different Kinds of Sowing

DAVID AND I spent our first four years together preaching, teaching, and doing graduate studies in multiple countries. Then our lives changed dramatically with the birth of our first daughter, Rebecca. Within three weeks it became apparent that this little one would be a strong-willed child. Back in Atlanta, where we were based at the time, I held her close as I rocked her in her nursery and prayed, "Jesus, help us! I need Your wisdom with this one!" It seemed that God was reassuring and smiling as He asked, "Why do you think I gave her to you and David?"

In weeks, David and I were back on the road with baby Becca. We visited a different city every week, and within four months, we were back overseas ministering. Travel and ministry were our lives, but I had no idea about the practicalities of adding a baby to our way of life. We discovered that in some Western nations nice dogs were welcome in nice restaurants, but nice babies were not. In contrast, people in Southern Asian cultures light up when they see a baby coming. They delight in them. Rebecca was carried proudly around countless restaurants by doting maître d's and up and down plane aisles by flight attendants.

In some cultures where people keep their distance from foreigners, especially Americans, strangers suddenly seemed to see David and me as more approachable after Becca was born. I loved being a mom (and still do!), and I found that having a little one opened hearts and relationships for ministry in ways David

Different Kinds of Sowing

and I had not imagined. There were a few challenges, which our friends met by loading extra suitcases with diapers and bringing them to India. But we just kept the ministry schedule going as much as possible with Becca in our arms or stroller, and all was well.

But by the time Rebecca was five months old I realized all was not well. I had been traveling with a baby from the time she was three weeks old. I tried to keep up the same pace of travel with David because I didn't want to let him down. But back home in the same rocking chair, I realized I was depleted. I was stressed by having a baby in public places and events constantly, and my weight was down to one hundred pounds. I sat and rocked Becca once more as tears ran down my cheeks.

I prayed, "Lord, I don't want to let You down, and I don't want to let David down. But I can't do this for Becca's sake or for mine. Somehow help me find a pace that's right and best for us all in this season. And Lord, please give me a deep peace so I can be a source of Your peace for my baby and for my husband." And God did. I wish I could say that was the last time I had to pray that prayer with tears. But He always met me at those points of desperately needed wisdom when our family's needs were changing.

One of those times was when Becca turned three. We were enrolled in language school, and I discovered I was pregnant with baby Jennifer. And I had one of those uncomfortable aha moments.

We were attending a Scottish Presbyterian church not far from our language school. On our first Sunday there I took Becca to the children's church and slipped back thirty minutes later to see how she was doing. Peeking in from the back door, I saw the missionary's daughter (mine!) receive the offering plate from the child next to her and hesitate. (Oh no.) I watched in horror as Rebecca slowly took some money out of the plate instead of putting money in.

Now, any three-year-old can do that. But when the child is a missionary kid—and David Grant, the legendary offering taker, is her father—well, you can imagine the terror that struck my heart! Fortunately (and embarrassingly), a children's staff member who was standing by ready to receive the plate saw what happened. She firmly passed the plate back to Becca and waited for her to reluctantly put the money back into it.

I slipped away and said, "Lord, we need to talk."

This child had been in a different church almost every week of her short life. She loved going into new nurseries and kids' churches and barely looked back at me to say goodbye when she did. But unfortunately, I observed that because she was always the guest preacher's daughter, everyone tended to defer to her. If there was a conflict, other children were encouraged to defer to Rebecca. After all, she would only be there that one time.

But in watching my daughter take money out of the offering plate, I also realized how many times she watched her dad take offerings and receive envelopes containing money from church leaders. In her young mind all the money taken during those offering services went to Dad. Some people gave offerings; some people received offerings—and we were receivers. This little girl had no idea that the money was going to support other missionaries from all over the world, as well as hundreds of new church plants and Bible schools in Southern Asia.

By lunchtime that day, I knew we had to make a change: We had to have a base to call home. We needed to be part of a local community of faith where our soon-to-be *two* daughters would have continuity and friends with whom they would learn to give as well as take. David would continue to be the missionary-evangelist God had called and gifted him to be on three continents, and I would become the still-called-of-God

Different Kinds of Sowing

mom who created a home and served in ministry locally with two little girls who needed to be mentored to follow Jesus too.

For the next ten years, our family served God's call based out of Brussels at the request of our regional director, legendary missionary Charles Greenaway. My husband served as the area director for Southern Asia, where residential visas were problematic. I was a part-time administrative assistant for him and later taught missions part-time at Continental Theological Seminary, while traveling with David and the girls three to four months of the year. Our church home was Christian Center, and that international faith community could not have been more supportive of our family, our different calling in life, and God's mission.

Was it hard? Yes. The first year was very hard for both David and me because we loved doing life and ministry together. My passion for God's mission and the people He loves still burned in my heart and went to them with David. But over the years, a healthy response to God's call cannot ignore practical realities of life and family. The call of God on my life included two daughters, and I was their only mom. They needed stability. And David would come home like a whirlwind. He needed someone to create a family space that included stability, peace, and a safe, listening ear to process the victories and challenges of intense ministry and leadership.

As David traveled in the United States to preach and represent the pressing needs in Southern Asia, and then as he stopped in Belgium to be with us on his way back to Southern Asia, it was never easy. When he arrived to preach there, he was sometimes teased about his "invisible" wife. But God helped us know it was wise and we could do it for a season. And where He leads, He gives grace. We found joy, stability, and fruitfulness.

Honestly, we didn't always get it right. Our children helped us know that—sometimes painfully. As Becca, Jennifer, and I had

53

breakfast each morning while David was traveling, Jennifer in particular would lament, "I miss Daddy. Why does he have to be gone so much?"

Becca, who was older and wiser at seven, answered impatiently, "You know, Jennifer! God called Daddy to be an evangelist and preach everywhere. He's doing what God called him to do."

But three-year-old Jennifer, looking indignantly at her, was not convinced. "I know that!" she said. *"But does God make his schedule?"*

Unexpected Gifts from God

When our girls were in childhood and their early teens, God opened doors for me to teach missions courses part-time at Continental Theological Seminary in Brussels and later at Southeastern University in Lakeland, Florida. Teaching cross-cultural courses to equip and inspire students from multiple countries to take Jesus to the nations became an active learning process and passion for me. God ignited a fire in my soul to foster classroom environments where we not only would learn about God and His Spirit intellectually but could welcome and experience Him and His Spirit—moving, speaking to, convicting, liberating, and empowering us.

It's by His Spirit that He quickens His Word, brings light to truth, and anoints teachers who are sensitive and welcome Him into their classrooms. I believe classrooms in Christian institutions where the Holy Spirit is fully welcome and allowed to lead should be the most dynamic and life-changing environments in the world. Where His fire burns, lives will be changed—even in doctoral classes! There's no need to choose between academic excellence and the ongoing, life-giving work of the Spirit. We desperately need both.

During this more hidden season for the girls and me, several

Different Kinds of Sowing

key mentors who were scholars, ministers, and men of God challenged and encouraged me to pursue a doctoral studies journey myself: Del Tarr, PhD, who at that time was president of the Assemblies of God Seminary and a professor of cultural anthropology; John Higgins, ThD, a theological scholar, friend, and missionary leader in education; and Ivan Satyavrata, PhD, another international church leader, scholar, and friend. As part of the growing ministry in Southern Asia and Europe, higher education was highly valued and a critically important strategy for equipping young men and women to build God's kingdom in their nations.

And so I began a doctoral program in intercultural education at Biola University School of Intercultural Studies. My focus was on Bible college and seminary education as strategic ministerial training to prepare effective, Spirit-empowered leaders for their specific cultural contexts. As doctoral programs tend to be, it was intense—and at times, isolating. But God led me to a topic in leadership that could be pursued in partnership with our closest national leaders and friends across Southern Asia. My research was not done alone; it was a collaborative effort to learn together how effective the expansive ministerial training efforts in the nations were at that time. And from my first phone call of inquiry, my adviser, Judy Lingenfelter, PhD, was a gift of God—a woman of excellence, scholarship, joy, and friendship over that doctoral journey.

I am forever indebted to the Southern Asian colleagues who took that journey with me and David. They generously gave their time to my research as I sought to understand how they view and practice leadership. They opened their classrooms, boardrooms, and prayer meetings with students to me. And when all the data was compiled after several years, we all had findings to celebrate: Southern Asia Bible College (SABC) was indeed preparing Pentecostal leaders for their national setting. But even more encouraging were the visible, documented indications the Holy Spirit was at work. Through courageous, Spirit-led academic leaders, God was challenging cultural leadership models that conflicted with His biblical principles for called leaders. SABC was indeed creating an educational environment that was developing ministerial students who looked more like Jesus, and it was developing ministry methods that resembled the early church in spirit and practice more than the traditional cultural leadership models reflecting other worldviews.

During that, again, more hidden time, God also began to grow a passion in me that would mark ministry seasons to come. In every college where I was welcomed to teach in India, Europe, and America, I began to see the hand of God for ministry on hundreds of young women. They were often timid, having sometimes been set apart physically in classrooms from the male students, or set apart in their hearts and minds by teachings that disavowed the calling they sensed on their own lives.

But miraculously, something God had been growing in my own life in the Spirit connected with what He was beginning to do in these young women's lives—first in one, then dozens, and over time hundreds. Courageous, God-seeking young women I met in France, Belgium, Ireland, Finland, Austria, Sri Lanka, Bangladesh, Germany, India, and the United States all seemed to just be waiting, standing on their spiritual toes to step up in obedience to the One who was calling them. He was pouring His anointing out on His daughters, as prophesied by the prophet Joel. I sensed my God-given role was to discern that movement among His daughters wherever I ministered, pray for His anointing on their lives, and challenge them to step up and into His sovereign call. No turning back!

Much of my charge calling those young women to spiritual arms was spoken in a whisper. That was often all I had left in my voice by the time I was able to pray with them one-on-one.

Different Kinds of Sowing

But the God who remains ever faithful, and who simply asked me to be available to Him, continued to orchestrate His good plans for daughters who heard His voice and were determined to obey Him.

Our Daughters Were Blessed Too

While Rebecca and Jennifer were growing up, David and I would move to a new mission base in a different nation every four years. That wasn't the plan, but that was how our journey in missions unfolded through different seasons. While neither of us would recommend that to others, it became a blessing not only to us but to our daughters. Only now, after Rebecca and Jennifer have become parents and missionaries themselves, do they realize more fully how God used aspects of their lives as missionary kids on three continents to help them become the women of faith and ministry they are today.

One of our greatest joys as their parents was introducing two babies, and then two little girls, to our Southern Asia family and friends who would become part of their lives. They and other wonderful, close missionary friends there warmly adopted our daughters into their hearts and homes. They fixed their favorite foods, the way grandmas and aunties do. Our Indian family helped them learn to walk, and because Becca loved animals and was very creative, they later helped find her stray goats and art supplies to use on kitchen tables and in hotel restaurants. By the time Jennifer turned three she was already addicted to ruffles, ribbons, and Indian bangles—so everywhere we went, our friends loved covering her little arms in more of them. (You can't have too many bangles!)

Years later, Rebecca would return to the same cities and families as a single young woman to work with Project Rescue, using the arts as therapy for women and girls who had previously been held as sexual slaves. Auntie Sheila Satyavrata, our dear friend and pastor's wife in whose home Rebecca was based, made sure Rebecca dressed appropriately for the street, suggested the best way to wear her hair, and, despite her twinkling eyes and chuckle, was always Becca's fierce protector. For both of our girls our Indian family always provided lots of truth with lots of love.

Similarly, American colleagues across the globe and associates in Europe loved our girls and invested in their lives like older sisters when we were based there. Several of them discerned and encouraged Rebecca's and Jennifer's different God-given gifts from an early age through their teens. Our dear friends strengthened our hands as parents.

Our family's growing-up season really was a time of sowing—but a different kind of sowing than ministers and missionaries often envision. David and I modified how we fulfilled God's call in order to sow more intentionally into our daughters' lives and spiritual formation. Instead of me sowing as we traveled constantly, seed sowing flowed naturally out of opportunities in cities we called home to invest in the lives of young people who were preparing for ministry and missions. Lastly, God gave me the humbling privilege to sow seeds of faith and courage for His call in more of His younger daughters than I could have imagined. Many of them now courageously sow seeds of faith and take Jesus around the world through evangelism, discipleship, pastoral ministries, and compassion ministries in their own nation and others.

Just to be clear, in all that time, David Grant was faithful to do what David Grant does: travel the world preaching Jesus and inspiring the global church to God's great mission. And in the process my husband, who was born to give, inspired thousands of churches and thousands of God's people to do the same.

LEFT: These are the prayer cards we distributed, asking people to intercede for our family.

RIGHT: This photo of Rebecca and Jennifer is from Christmas in Kolkata, India, and the girls were all dressed to go to the traditional Christmas morning service at Kolkata Mission.

Anita Koeshall, PhD, is a great friend, peer mentor, and missionary colleague. She and I were in some of the same doctoral studies and later both taught in the Intercultural Studies PhD Program at the Assemblies of God Theological Seminary.

ABOVE: Me praying for women in one of the Project Rescue Southern Asia programs
LEFT: Judy Lingenfelter, PhD, my doctoral adviser and friend, hooding me at graduation from the Intercultural Education PhD Program at Biola University in 1999

Part II

Navigating Change
and
Growth

Chapter 7

Harems, Servant Leaders, and Little Kings

WHEN DAVID AND I met, there was one area of life and ministry on which we were miles apart: our perspectives on politics.

Growing up outside Washington, DC, some aspects of secular politics were intriguing to me. But when it came to anything political relating to the church, I was dismayed. And the man I married? He danced with it! Never an avoider of conflict, tension, or relational intrigue, David Grant, like his dad, Curtis, relished the give-and-take of organizational and denominational politics—in the church and out. So for years as David danced, I happily sat it all out in the shadows.

Then God used two very different experiences as catalysts to challenge my perspective on political dynamics and my assumptions about the parameters of His call. At the time, God was stretching my understanding and practice of Jesus-modeled servant leadership in political contexts for the realities of an increasingly multicultural church and world.

First, David and I had the opportunity to visit Istanbul for a World Missions leadership team meeting. We were given a tour of the stunning Topkapi Palace, which was the royal residence of the sultans of the Ottoman Empire for almost four hundred years. That tour included a visit to the famous Imperial Harem, which has more than four hundred rooms that at one time housed the sultan's mother and more than a thousand concubines, eunuchs, wives, servants, and children simultaneously. It is such a magnificent place, both architecturally and artistically! But when you learn that women in the harem were under lockdown 24/7, you begin to get a clearer, far less romanticized picture. Imagine three hundred to four hundred of some of the most beautiful, chosen women in the world all in one place in lockdown together for years—all vying daily for the attention and favor of one powerful man. That is not a pretty picture!

Our visit to the Imperial Harem led me to do some research on Middle Eastern harems, which ultimately led me back to the biblical story of Esther. Rather than the romanticized image depicted by European painters of one powerful sultan eating fruit offered by one beautiful, submissive woman, traditional Middle Eastern harems were in reality some of the most dangerous, political, violent—and, yes, sexually exploitative—places in the world. Women who were privileged to be chosen for a sultan's harem represented political interests, competing kingdoms, hoped-for alliances, and agendas with the highest of stakes. As a result, murder, poisoning, and other forms of treachery were commonplace.

And the more I learned about the Middle Eastern harem, the more an assumption I held about God and His call on my life came into question.

From my teen years I was deeply stirred by the story of Esther, a daughter of God living in exile who was orphaned and then chosen to become a member of the Persian king's harem. It's an oft-told story and favorite of many women called of God: Esther finds favor with the king, so he makes her queen (the most influential woman). Ultimately, she's willing to risk her life by

Harems, Servant Leaders, and Little Kings

using her influence with him to save her people, God's people. God indeed raised Esther up for such a moment in history.

But I had handily passed by the details: In the process of Esther becoming queen and saving God's people, He chose a path for her that required her to become immersed in a harem, one of the most sexual, violent, and political environments on earth.

You may be thinking, "But God gave her favor!" Yes, He did. And Esther wisely accepted the counsel of a eunuch who stepped up and coached her through that specific environment he knew so well. But sometimes because humanity is human (and often when the stakes are high), being the favored one can be the most dangerous thing of all. Not all those women in the harem loved Esther or wished her well. She still had to witness and navigate a treacherous, sensual, political environment step-by-step. And she had to do it without knowing the end of the story, as we do. God had a sovereign plan for Esther, but there was an unusual process of preparation she had to go through in order to use her life and influence.

In God's mysterious ways, He used the story of Esther and insights concerning the path He ordained her to walk in order to deeply challenge my own understanding of His call on my life. I clearly sensed His hand on my life "for such a time as this." But whenever I encountered an environment or culture within the church that seemed overtly political, I always said to myself, "God would never lead me there."

How foolish of me. Looking back on the great stories of Scripture through a political lens, it's clear that God led Moses, Joseph, Deborah, David, Mary, and Paul to fulfill His redemptive purposes in highly politicized environments, literally, as well as religious ones. Jesus Himself was born into a politically charged world where it was dangerous to live out the will of His Father. And the redeemed of the ages will rejoice together with Him in heaven because He walked it out—all the way to the cross. How could I naively assume God would make exceptions for me when He had called me to go wherever and do whatever He would choose?

My comfort level with political dynamics, or any other kind of dynamic, was not a priority for God. The question was whether this daughter was willing to continue to say yes and remain available to Him over a lifetime of serving in whatever environments He sovereignly chose for me. And could I do so with integrity, grace, His presence, and courage?

During my doctoral studies I was taught an anthropological definition for *political dynamics* in culture. For me that was very helpful. Broadly stated, it is simply that *political dynamics* are not restricted to official state institutions or the formal power structures we typically consider to be political; rather, they reference "how people manage their everyday social relations through persuasion, force, violence, and control over resources."[1] So in that broader definition, whenever and wherever people are working together in any context, including Christian ones, political dynamics will be a byproduct. Even if a group of five university students is assigned to a group project, whether a leader is appointed or chosen or not, over time one will ultimately emerge. Political dynamics in human interaction and the use of power and authority in some form are essential parts of life, community, organizations, and governments—and even the function of a church.

In the process of my research, "Help me understand" became one of the guiding statements of my life. Jesus was leading me to step into new cultures and environments, not as a teacher first but as a sincere learner. If I want to genuinely love the people to whom Jesus has called us, it's critical to understand their cultures (or subcultures in our own nations), their stories, and yes, why they do what they do in their political environments. Over the

Harems, Servant Leaders, and Little Kings

years, I've found most people to be gracious and even grateful when someone who is new in ministry or leadership cares enough to sincerely say, "Help me understand."

Some of the most helpful conclusions that emerged from my studies, integrated with forty-five years of working with colleagues in leadership across multiple settings, are summarized here in this chapter.

Our ministry takes place in many cultures that have different, complex political dynamics—inside and outside the church, and even if we'd never left our country of birth. If you ask church leaders to describe the qualities of *biblical leadership* or *servant leadership*, you will likely receive traditional biblical responses that every good follower of Jesus knows we *should* believe: Be a person of prayer, a person of the Word who loves and cares for people, a person of integrity, and so on.

But after that, if pressed, leaders' responses tend to reflect their culture's definition of *good* or *effective* leadership more than a biblical one. It's very human, and it's impossible not to be shaped by the values of our birth cultures. And the ways people in the church view good or poor leadership are no exception.

After many years of working as an anthropologist and missiology scholar, Sherwood Lingenfelter, PhD, concluded that every culture is its own "prison of disobedience."[2] That does not mean all cultures don't have good and admirable traits. But his contention is that over time, all people groups collectively develop systems of finance, economics, social relations, religion, and so on. Without God and the influence of His Word and Spirit those systems tend to become more and more humanly self-serving, potentially exploiting the vulnerable and abusing power. In a word, any culture without God's influence through God's people will perpetuate certain kinds of sin. Without the transformational power of the gospel at work through God's Word and His people, a church will not only look like the culture in which it was birthed, but it will tolerate—and can even perpetuate—the sins of its surrounding secular culture as well.

As we share Jesus around the world, the goal isn't to encourage people or churches to be more like the American church or any other cultural church. Rather, we welcome them to follow the One who gave His life to save us from our sins and transform us by the power of His Spirit. That life-changing, miraculous journey does not make those individuals or churches more like us or more like the best of *our* culture and church. Amazingly, choosing Jesus and becoming His lifetime followers will always make people more like Him—wherever and whatever their starting point.

You may be thinking, "Beth, this is a tangent." I don't think so. As men and women of God who are leaders, we must continually embrace His Word's convicting power and the Holy Spirit's transforming work personally in order to become less molded by our cultural leadership models and more like Jesus-hearted, people-loving, power-releasing servants. If we are not intentionally committed to His work in us, we will inevitably—and easily—fall more into our culture's leadership models than the one provided by the God we've been called to humbly serve.

To apply this truth in real time, I must often ask myself an uncomfortable question: Does my voice or message sound more like my secular culture's voice and political talking points, or does it sound more like the prophetic voice and message of John the Baptist crying in the wilderness, "Make straight the way for the Lord" (John 1:23)?

Paul's very familiar words in Romans 12 have pertinent meaning for this spiritual task:

> Therefore, I urge you, brothers and sisters, in view of
> God's mercy, to offer your bodies as a living sacrifice,

Harems, Servant Leaders, and Little Kings

> holy and pleasing to God—this is your true and proper worship. Do not conform to the pattern of this world [cultural patterns that are not aligned with God's Word and will], but be transformed by the renewing of your mind. Then you will be able to test and approve what God's will is—his good, pleasing and perfect will.
> —ROMANS 12:1–2

Every human culture, organization, denomination, or church has political dynamics in the broader definition. That includes the way decisions are made, how those with authority use their power, and how the appropriate uses of power, relationships, and resources are defined. These processes are essential for the organizations to function. We do not need to avoid them but can have spiritual influence on them as we walk out God's call within those spheres. God can give us wisdom and insight to navigate them for His glory. We can influence them by His Spirit and gifts as we walk in these spaces, sensitive and prayerfully asking, "God, what is happening here? How can I best serve You, Your church, Your people, and Your purposes here?" (My dear husband smiled wryly as he read this, thinking, "Of course!")

There is great news to celebrate. One can find Jesus-like servant leaders in some of the most authoritarian and the most egalitarian cultures in the world, sometimes where we may not expect to see them. In churches where the Spirit of the Lord is welcome and at work and where sons and daughters are hungry to seek Him first, you can find humble servant leaders who look disarmingly like Jesus. The strengths of their respective human cultures remain, but one can see visible evidence of the Holy Spirit's inimitable work, His spiritual gifts and fruit in godly women and men in the church globally. My heart cries out to God to be one of that number!

But there are also realities to grieve. One can find little kings in leadership in the body of Christ as well—including in more egalitarian cultures where philosophically all people are equal, and in cultures that are traditionally more hierarchical. The good news of the gospel is that Jesus still forgives sin and still breaks the chains of bondage when anyone, including ministers and church leaders, repents and throws themself upon God's mercy. Culturally exploitative, abusive leadership patterns can be challenged and broken, just as any addiction or form bondage can. But they are next to impossible to break without doing the hard spiritual work of submission to the Spirit's conviction of sin and embracing His transforming Word and work in our lives. This journey will absolutely keep us on our knees. As ministers and leaders, we too are desperate for repentance, God's forgiveness, and His amazing grace. Thankfully, as John 8:36 tells us, those whom the Spirit sets free are free indeed!

In conclusion, like all the men and women of God who have gone before us, we find ourselves in a complicated world riddled with powerful political dynamics. Some are empowering and just; some are disempowering and unjust. But this is the world to which God calls us, His people, to navigate with wisdom, integrity, courage, and pure hearts. He asks us to fully submit to His leadership, saying, "Yes, Lord, if that is Your will, I will go." The *wherever* may be culturally and politically different than we expect, but God is still able to do "exceedingly abundantly above all that we ask or think, according to the power that works in us" (Eph. 3:20, WEB).

Who knew that a visit to the Topkapi Palace harem, revisiting Esther's story, and doctoral studies on leadership would challenge my understanding of God's call and mysterious ways? God did. And through it He was preparing my heart and mind for where He would lead in the years to come. He is so graciously faithful.

Harems, Servant Leaders, and Little Kings

QUESTIONS FOR REFLECTION

1. Reflect on your thoughts and emotions about political environments as contexts for fulfilling the call of God to ministry. When God called me, I had assumptions about them that were challenged through my experiences and God's Word. Have you consciously or subconsciously put conditions on your yes to serve Jesus anywhere? Consider the political environments in which God sovereignly raised up Moses, Joseph, and Deborah to serve His redeeming purposes.

2. In what way, if any, has this chapter challenged or inspired your thinking about Esther's journey from being a young Jewish woman, orphaned and living in exile from her homeland, to becoming King Xerxes' queen of Persia? What are some important lessons that contemporary men and women of God can glean from how she navigated the circumstances that could have cost her life?

3. How do you define the qualities of an effective leader? How does your description align with the biblical concept of Jesus, the servant leader? In what way does your description align with your secular culture's values for leadership? Identify areas of tension between those models. Pray about growing into greater alignment with the direction and image of Jesus, who laid down His life to seek and to save the lost.

4. Reflecting on Sherwood Lingenfelter's concept of culture as a "prison of disobedience," identify ways that your own secular culture's values directly conflict with the Word of God. To what extent do

they hinder the work and fruit of the Spirit in your personal life and in your life as a minister, pastor, or leader? Prayerfully seek God's help in each area for the Spirit's liberating, transforming work.

5. A larger anthropological definition of political dynamics, as presented in this chapter, can be helpful in understanding and navigating our present political contexts as ministers and leaders. Rather than simply reacting emotionally to politics, consider some practical ways the people of God can navigate political environments wisely, redemptively, and as missionaries for the greater work of His kingdom.

6. Prayerfully reflect on Mordecai's challenging question to Esther:

> For if you remain silent at this time, relief and deliverance for the Jews will arise from another place, but you and your father's family will perish. And who knows but that you have come to your royal position for such a time as this?
>
> —ESTHER 4:14

What has God positioned you for in His divine purposes in this time and season? Is there a specific way (or ways) in which He has called you to use your voice that you are avoiding or neglecting? Pray for courage to act and to speak prophetically as God leads.

7. Whatever their position or platform, we are called to help younger men and women develop into servant-hearted leaders who emulate Jesus rather than becoming "little kings or queens" who use power to maintain their personal position and authority. Without intentionality on the parts of mentors and

Harems, Servant Leaders, and Little Kings

spiritual leaders to disciple Jesus-hearted leaders, a younger generation will inevitably reflect their secular culture's leaders. What are some ways we can intentionally mentor younger people to become more like Him, as outlined in Philippians 2?

Topkapi Palace in Istanbul, Turkey

Inside the Topkapi Palace harem in Istanbul, Turkey

Chapter 8

Breaking Ground for Hope

ONE NIGHT, DAVID received a call from a colleague named Devaraj. We didn't know it at the time, but that call would alter the trajectory of our yes to Jesus. Devaraj had established a ministry among young men who were addicted to drugs in a city of twenty million people. He had seen plenty of hard things. But on that particular night, Devaraj was weeping. He had taken his outreach team into the city's infamous red-light district only blocks away from his base.

There, they discovered block after block of multistory brothels where women and girls were being sold for sex. Some were as young as eleven and twelve years of age, being raped multiple times, night after night, by men who were paying their madame or pimp. This horrifying city within a city was home to an estimated one hundred thousand sexually exploited women and children.

In the middle of that epicenter of evil Devaraj boldly stood on the street and shared the story of Jesus over a public address system. It was the story of God's Son, who loved us so much that He came to earth to save us from evil and give us all new life. And from the crowded streets and brothels more than a hundred women got word to him that they wanted to follow this Jesus, but they were literally slaves. They had been sold into this slavery—often as young girls, many of them from the little nation of Nepal. They literally could not leave, but they asked if

75

LEADING WITH A WHISPER

our friend would take their little daughters to a place of safety, where they could be spared from that same slavery.

Through tears on the other end of the line Devaraj asked, "Brother David, can we take thirty-seven little girls and create a place of safety for them?"

I listened as my husband said without hesitation, "Sure, Devaraj! No problem!"

In that second, David and I both knew that those little girls— who ranged from the ages of three to twelve, having been born in brothels to mothers who were being held in slavery—were precious to God. He knew them by name, and He loved them. Here was a moment of opportunity to get them out of this hell where they were clearly at risk, if not already being victimized. How could we not act?

Then the visionary in our family (David) turned over and went to sleep, and the planner among us (that would be me) stayed awake in the dark, wondering, "How in the world are we going to do this?"

Without a plan, a strategy, or even any real working knowledge we began working with Devaraj as he found a couple of apartments, and women from local churches volunteered to become housemothers to the young girls who were given to this "uncle" and his team. And with a very steep learning curve Project Rescue, a ministry to sexually exploited women and children in Southern Asia, was born.

At the time, David served as area director for our organization for Southern Asia. So as soon as we made the decision personally to begin what was then considered an out-on-the-edge ministry to women in prostitution, he called a meeting with all our area personnel. David shared what had just happened and our personal decision to follow God through this new open door for His mission.

The room full of global workers was quiet; David asked if they

76

Breaking Ground for Hope

had any input. Then Brother Andrew McCabe—who had been born on the mission field to Scottish parents serving in India, and had later returned there for a lifetime of service—began to speak.

"Brother David, I believe this is God," he said. "But I feel I must warn you. In all my years in Southern Asia this evil is closest to the heart of hell. I believe we should do this. But know in doing so, all hell will break lose. Brother Grant, this could cost us everything, but I believe this is God's heart. I'm with you."

David and I left that meeting soberly committed to proceed while trusting God for whatever lay ahead.

Our family then had to head straight from there to the airport because Rebecca, Jennifer, and I had to begin the long journey back to our home in Belgium. David was going to remain in Southern Asia for further meetings. But as our hotel shuttle navigated the crowded city streets, I spotted a little boy stepping out from the curb directly into our path. To our relief, he ran quickly and was able to make it to the other side. But to our horror, his little sister followed right after him into the traffic. And suddenly, despite our driver's screeching attempt to stop, there was a horrible sound as our vehicle hit the little girl...and stopped.

Immediately, people in that city of multiplied millions who rarely see justice began to run angrily toward our vehicle. It's not uncommon for foreigners involved in an accident to be mobbed and their cars set on fire. The conventional wisdom is to keep driving if you want to escape with your life—but that's not what we did. As people were rushing toward our car, I pushed Rebecca and Jennifer down onto the floorboard and began to call out loud, "Jesus! Jesus! Jesus!" My husband got out of the car to go to the little girl, and I prayed silently, "Oh, God, don't let this be the end!"

Suddenly, the crowd of people who had been running toward

our car in anger stopped where they were. My husband returned and got in the car.

"David, where's the little girl?" I asked, bewildered.

"She's over there, running toward her parents," he said. "She's fine. There is no mark on her, no bruise—nothing. She jumped up immediately and ran."

He continued in wonder, "There was an elderly Hindu man standing on the median closest to the car. He said to me, 'Sir, you have just seen God.'"

Never in our lives had David and I seen God so blatantly cancel the natural consequences of a disaster in the making. It was literally a miracle.

For Project Rescue as a ministry and our family personally, that was Satan's first shot over the bow. Clearly, as Brother Andrew had warned, our decision to challenge this evil of sexual slavery and bring freedom to the women and children Jesus died for would entail greater spiritual battles than we had experienced to that point. And it would cost us. But amazingly, as our colleague's team began going into the red-light district every week to minister and pray, God began to work in those women's and children's lives.

In our first makeshift home of hope the little daughters of prostituted women were already being delivered from demonic power. Some of them had been offered to specific goddesses at birth, but they received Jesus, whom they'd never heard of before, with childlike faith. They were learning to follow Jesus, and many were filled with the Holy Spirit. Soon, mothers who were still being held in exploitation had young daughters praying for them daily in the Spirit. Over time, some of those mothers followed their daughters out of bondage as they witnessed the love their daughters received and how they were flourishing as part of God's family.

While Devaraj was quickly building staff to develop the ministry to the children and outreach to their mothers, David immediately began to make contacts back in the US to share this urgent new ministry with friends and churches and to begin raising funds for it. At the same time, he connected with pastors in Southern Asia, shared the news with them, and asked them to pray about getting involved.

The response to the news of this new ministry was strongly positive among many of our leaders and church friends. To an extent and with an urgency we did not anticipate, many began to give toward Project Rescue after promptly meeting with their church and missions boards. Checks began to flow into the Assemblies of God headquarters for Project Rescue.

But suddenly, while the ministry in Southern Asia was just getting off the ground, we started getting more questions than we had answers for. News travels quickly. But pioneering new ministries in areas that are controlled by organized crime, involve thousands of victims of sexual violence and exploitation, and generate massive local and national income must be developed prayerfully—one day and one step at a time. Much was at stake.

While David was preaching and raising funds, I felt a spiritual responsibility to prayerfully discern and articulate how this God-birthed ministry was going to fit theologically and missiologically with our denominational directives. David was making and receiving calls day and night on behalf of Project Rescue; I was in Scripture and creating diagrams to communicate how it fit into the mandate Jesus gave in Luke 4:18–19, into the Great Commission, and then into the "Four Pillars" our parent

LEADING WITH A WHISPER

organization was using at the time: reaching, teaching, planting, and offering compassion. We knew that some of our leaders and colleagues were concerned that we were going off the deep end of compassion and losing focus on evangelism, discipleship, and church planting. But from Devaraj's ministry to the pioneers who would follow in other cities, there was great intentionality across the board to ground this initiative in the love and whole mission of the God who had called us to it.

From the beginning, patterns of ministry began to emerge as God's Word and Spirit led. Prayer walking and intercession immediately became vital components; as workers brought their own care and God's tangible presence to dark, red-light district streets week after week, month after month, they built relationships with mothers and children. Project Rescue workers stood out in places of violent exploitation because they treated women and children with dignity, as sons and daughters God created in His image. Prayers of faith in Jesus' name were prayed with deeply wounded—sometimes dying—women lying behind soiled curtains in the heart of hell. Even there, we learned that God hears and answers the prayers of those who call upon His name.

It didn't take long for me to personally experience the strong emotions that are common when engaging with the victims of such horrible injustice—the anger of seeing a seven-year-old girl die after being strapped to a table and gang raped, or a little girl burned with cigarettes by her mother's "customer" to intimidate her into silence, or a woman running naked through the streets because her mind could no longer handle the trauma of being raped hour after hour. But it was critical that Project Rescue was not driven by these feelings. Those emotions are human, but they can become unhealthy and lead to anger and even hatred for those who enslave and exploit the vulnerable; after all, those who exploit others are also men and women Jesus loves and

Breaking Ground for Hope

came to save. We needed to be able to clearly articulate a biblical framework for Project Rescue in order to faithfully minister from God's love, as well as from the clear commands of His life-changing Word and mission.

Thankfully, when we do what God has called us to do in the ways He has called us to do it, with His Word and in the power of His Spirit, God does what He has promised to do. Women and children in places of horrific evil decided to follow Jesus. They were brought into a safe place to begin a new life, receiving medical care to deal with their very serious health issues and intervention to deal with the effects of trauma. In time, we developed programs to teach them literacy and job skills so they could leave prostitution behind for good. They learned immediately to pray, to worship God, and to receive the power of the Holy Spirit.

The new homes became remarkable places of new life. They were marked by deliverance, joy, healings, and life-changing hope. Project Rescue grew into a ministry of the whole gospel for the whole person. Granted, the context for the work was dramatic and something the church often considered taboo as a context for ministry. But the One who is not willing that any should perish was reaching by His Spirit through faithful outreach workers and was redeeming women and their children out of great darkness and into His glorious light. Jesus was being proclaimed, newly redeemed sons and daughters were being discipled, and God's kingdom was being built—one former slave at a time.

God continues to raise up younger generations of men and women to work with sexually exploited women and children through Project Rescue ministries. By 2025 He has opened doors and ministry partnerships in forty-two cities across sixteen nations. Through 360-related programs staff minister to victims and survivors with outreaches and ongoing initiatives in areas known for prostitution. The thirty-six homes of hope that now span the global Project Rescue network provide holistic healing for victims—caring for their bodies, minds, and spirits, as well as providing vocational training and education to help them build new lives with dignity.

Hope has come full circle. Some of the young girls who were rescued twenty to twenty-five years ago in Southern Asia and in the last decade across Europe have now been called by God into this liberating ministry themselves. They were educated and now serve as staff to rescue and help restore other women and children. I've watched prayerfully with thanksgiving as these former victims go back into areas where they themselves were once enslaved and exploited. But now, they courageously go as part of a committed team to rescue and give hope to young girls and women still in bondage. These daughters are no longer victims; they are survivors who have become strong, Spirit-empowered, courageous women of God.

Adamma is one such survivor. She is a beautiful young woman from Nigeria. She was deceived into going to Spain to work as a nanny and was told she would be paid a good salary there. Traffickers told her she could pay back her debt for the travel to Europe and then send money to her impoverished family in Nigeria.

She was taken on a perilous journey through northern Africa that lasted for months, where she endured hunger, illness, and violence. Along the way, Adamma was beaten and raped.

After traveling by boat from Libya to Italy, she finally arrived

Breaking Ground for Hope

in Spain and discovered the real reason she had been taken there: to be sold into sexual slavery.

"What could I do?" she cried as she told her story. "They said I had to pay back €50,000 [$61,000 at the time] for the journey, and if I didn't, they would kill my family and me."

Adamma was constantly submitted to beatings, threats, and voodoo rituals. At one point she became pregnant and was drugged so she would miscarry. The bleeding was so heavy she almost died.

One day, Spanish police found Adamma lying on the side of the road and referred her to the Project Rescue home in Madrid. She was scared, traumatized, and in need of physical, emotional, and spiritual healing.

But in that home of hope Adamma received loving care, trauma counseling, and medical assistance—and a new family. As a result of her life-changing relationship with Jesus, she is now a new woman confident in who she is in Christ. Adamma has been baptized, has learned Spanish, and is now taking a social mediation course to continue to work with Project Rescue as a staff member. She is part of a local church. She is passionate about helping girls who have suffered the same horror she did find genuine healing and freedom.

There is a saying: Faces don't lie. Adamma's face reflects her joy in knowing Jesus and experiencing freedom in Him.

Over the last twenty-eight years, our Project Rescue leaders and staff team have been constantly humbled, amazed, and so very grateful to see what the Lord can do!

After that initial meeting in 1997 with other ministry leaders about beginning Project Rescue, the potentially disastrous car accident, and God's miraculous intervention, Rebecca, Jennifer,

LEADING WITH A WHISPER

and I ended up in a transit hotel for a night between flights back to Belgium.

But in the middle of the night I suddenly sat straight up in bed, wakened by the sound of heavy wooden hangers banging against each other in the closet.

I flipped the lights on and called out, "Who's there?"

Immediately, the noise stopped. But a heavy sense of threatening darkness remained. I threw open the door to the closet—and a dark shadow came out. I watched as it moved across the room to the heavy curtains at the window and stayed there.

My go-to is always to eliminate natural possibilities first. So while the girls huddled close together on the bed, big-eyed, I called the front desk.

"I think we have a rat," I said.

"No problem, ma'am!" the cheerful desk clerk replied. "A man will come with a towel."

Hmm. A towel didn't seem like it was going to cut it in this situation. So I simply said, "Thank you!" and hung up the phone.

The girls and I were obviously on high alert. So I joined them on the bed, where we sat in a circle and held hands. I prayed for God's protection over us and for the powers of darkness to go. Then, as if on cue, fifteen-year-old Becca began to softly sing "Ancient of Days" with her eyes closed. It is a song that we all knew well about God's mighty power. In a few moments Jennifer and I joined in, and together our voices began to get stronger and more confident. As we sang in praise to the Ancient of Days, His very presence began to fill that room, and the dark sense of foreboding emanating from the shadow began to lift.

A few minutes later the man from downstairs came with a towel and beat the curtains. Of course, there was no rat. (Unfortunately, rats are very common in India and Southern

Breaking Ground for Hope

Asia—in hotels, restaurants, streets, public meeting places, and so on.)

For the next twenty-four hours as the girls and I traveled on, one intimidating event after another occurred. For example, when we arrived at the international airport, we found that the agent who was to meet us at the counter and facilitate our check-in and departure had been replaced by someone else who seemed intent on making our departure more difficult, if not impossible. When we finally boarded the plane, we encountered a flight attendant with a similar attitude who reacted very negatively and rudely to me. Rebecca and Jennifer felt the aggression toward me in both cases and said, "Nobody reacts to you that way, Mom." Privately, it felt as if the presence of the Lord that had so tangibly covered us in the hotel experience was at war with the spirit of darkness that was very much at work in some of the people around us. There was a visceral reaction I could only attribute to spiritual confrontation.

When we were finally set to board the plane on the last leg of our journey, our flight was delayed due to incoming storms. Then at the last minute, it was cleared, and we hurried to board. And the plane headed into the gathering dark.

Yes, I'm intrigued by storms, but not flying into them with the plane shaking like a leaf. "Why are we even taking off?" we wondered. Amazingly, since Rebecca and Jennifer were already into the second night of travel with little sleep, they fell asleep beside me as soon as we boarded—and my mother heart breathed a silent prayer. "Thank You, Jesus, that they are at rest. Please help them stay asleep. And, Lord, please make a way through this storm and bring us safely home."

The bizarre intimidation from the enemy of God and His mission was unmistakable. But God covered and protected the girls and me that night—and we found later, He would do so along every step of the journey in the years to come.

85

LEADING WITH A WHISPER

Many people have asked me how I felt about exposing our daughters to such a dark world of sexual violence. When we first began that work, Rebecca was fifteen and Jennifer was twelve. But from our girls' early childhood, we were all together for much of our ministry.

They had ridden in cars and walked through Southern Asian streets since they were little. Real life happens on sidewalks in much of the world. Poverty, disease, death, homelessness, and even demonic power have nowhere to hide. So from childhood our daughters were asking hard questions that we then had to ask God to help us answer wisely, biblically, and compassionately. David and I tried to take those moments as opportunities to describe God's love, missionary heart, and redeeming intentions for every person we saw. We knew God was reaching for everyone around us. Were we?

The first time we took our girls through a massive red-light district at night, they were silent as they saw girls their own ages lining the dark streets. Just outside our car windows we could see their young faces and the cold darkness in their eyes. Young girls obediently lined up, waiting to be sold to the men approaching them. It's a horror that's unimaginable, and one you never forget.

As parents, David and I tried not to give our daughters details they didn't need; we just underscored the hope that is in Jesus. The contrast between the aggressive, suffocating evil they felt on the streets and the vibrant hope, love, and prayers they witnessed in the new homes of hope with girls who had been rescued was unforgettable. Satan is brutal and destructive. God is love, and His purposes are to redeem and restore. He reaches for the most vulnerable with compassion. Our daughters watched Project Rescue ministry pioneers reflect and live out those very Jesus-like qualities in the face of Satan's intimidating

86

Breaking Ground for Hope

power. Whether we were in Southern Asia, Europe, or America, we could not hide them from all darkness and evil. But we could equip and empower them with God's truth and the courage to challenge the darkness on behalf of those Jesus loves! Rebecca and Jennifer knew we did not cross oceans to keep our distance from the broken. We wanted to come close, the way Jesus does. (See Appendix A, "Practical Ways to Mentor Children to Act Compassionately Toward Victims of Exploitation.")

The ministry of Project Rescue made the best case to them for why we believe in and desperately need the power of the Holy Spirit. If we follow God's mission with our families, taking His light to those in darkness in our communities and cities, they will quickly realize that evil is not a concept; it's horribly real. And in our human strength we as Jesus followers don't have sufficient power to overcome evil and help people in bondage find freedom and deliverance. Suddenly, our children will experience with us the need to pray, "Oh, God, we are hungry and desperate for Your supernatural power and anointing. Without Your power this woman, this child, this man will not be free of Satan's chains. We cannot talk the enslaved out of bondage! Fill us with Your Spirit, Lord, with everything You have promised You would give us to carry out Your life-changing mission! With You and by Your Spirit we can do all things! In Jesus' powerful name we pray, amen!"

Sound doctrine concerning the Holy Spirit is important. I've never seen doctrine create a great hunger for the fullness of the Spirit, but what does is encouraging a younger generation to join us side by side in the great mission of God for which the Spirit of Pentecost correctly reframes our seeking of Him.

The power of Pentecost detached from the Great Commission can unfortunately make the outpouring of the Holy Spirit upon His sons and daughters seem optional, an arbitrary personal choice from a menu of spiritual experiences. We do not, cannot,

87

and will not see God's miraculous redemption, rescue, and restoration of people set free from dark bondage without His power!

Our daughters have seen the horrors of darkness. But more importantly they have seen the greater hope and light of Jesus. They too grew to know and walk in the power and presence of the all-powerful God.

Jesus is the One who proclaimed and promised,

> All authority in heaven and on earth has been given to me. Therefore go and make disciples of all nations, baptizing them in the name of the Father and of the Son and of the Holy Spirit, and teaching them to obey everything I have commanded you. And surely I am with you always, to the very end of the age.
>
> —MATTHEW 28:18–20

QUESTIONS FOR REFLECTION

1. Read Isaiah 59:4, 14–15:

> No one calls for justice; no one pleads a case with integrity. They rely on empty arguments, they utter lies; they conceive trouble and give birth to evil....So justice is driven back, and righteousness stands at a distance; truth has stumbled in the streets, honesty cannot enter. Truth is nowhere to be found, and whoever shuns evil becomes a prey. The LORD looked and was displeased that there was no justice.

In very violent places in our cities and nations today, evil and injustice are ravaging lives. But as the prophet Isaiah says, truth is being tragically ravaged as well on those very streets. Exploitation begins with lies, is perpetuated by lies, and tragically ends in lies and death.

Breaking Ground for Hope

Unless God's people stand up to bring His liberating truth to those places and introduce the people living in them to the One who will never betray or mislead them—because He Himself is truth—injustice, evil, and violence will continue, woefully unchallenged.

Consider the crisis of truth in your own culture and context. What are some ways that God's people can discern the lies of the enemy and speak truth in love to redeem and restore those who have lost hope and been victimized by injustice and violence? God stood up with His salvation, righteousness, and redemption. How can we stand up as well and best represent Him to the broken?

2. In John 4:1–42 the writer recounts the well-known story of Jesus' encounter with a Samaritan woman at the town well. Read the story through the lens of the following questions:

   - What words would you use to describe how Jesus approached this woman, who went alone to the well at midday? What was His demeanor toward her compared to the disciples'? How would men in her village have treated her?

   - What are some indicators of the Samaritan woman's shame?

   - When the woman at first did not fully disclose her story to Jesus, He spoke the truth of her way-too-complicated sexual history. What was His ultimate purpose in sharing His knowledge of her personal story?

89

- At times, the concept of speaking truth to people who have very painful and shameful pasts (and presents) is viewed as a spiritual responsibility to "make sure they know they're in sin." Was that Jesus' intent? We know that the way in which He spoke this woman's truth made her realize He was a prophet, but He did not add to her shame. If He had, He would have been like every other man she knew. In what ways were His accurate statements to her noteworthy?

- Consider this passage through the lens of the chapter title, "Breaking Ground for Hope." Reflect on practical ways in which we, like Jesus, can speak truth redemptively to those who are in bondage and without hope, from our neighbors to the nations. Ask yourself: What does hope sound like in my voice? What does shaming sound like in my voice? Am I, by my very tone, shaming the hopeless and those in bondage? Or am I breaking spiritual ground for hope and faith to begin to grow in their hearts and lives, which will lead them to freedom in Jesus?

Rev. Huldah Buntain and me breaking ground for a new home of hope for daughters whose mothers are involved in prostitution

Women in the red-light district are attending the red-light district church. The spiritual journey to freedom often begins here before the physical journey to freedom is possible.

This is a Project Rescue–affiliated school of excellence and hope for children born in brothels. These children are future doctors, teachers, social workers, and staff for ministries like Project Rescue.

Adamma is now a joyful, confident woman of God. She is in training and serving as staff to help bring hope, healing, and new life to other victims of trafficking.

Chapter 9

A Voice for God's Daughters

PROJECT RESCUE'S EARLY years introduced us to a whole new world of cruel systems of injustice and abuses of power. Whenever an outreach worker connected with an individual child or woman in prostitution, the very dark system in which she was enslaved rose up and pushed back. Politics? What we had experienced before was elementary compared to the crushing systems of sexual slavery that have existed for centuries in cities around the world. Local leaders warned us privately that attempting to bring any change in those red-light districts would be very dangerous, if not impossible. In multiple nations sexual exploitation was connected to the highest levels of government and was a major source of income to political leaders.

But in the middle of the intense spiritual battles that followed, we were amazed to see God's grace at work in women's and children's lives. Like Nehemiah's workers rebuilding the wall around their beloved city, Project Rescue staff learned to build this ministry with one hand and always be ready to do spiritual warfare with the other. Our network ministry teams in different cities—and later, nations—were experiencing the reality that with God and in His Spirit all things, even the miracles they needed, were indeed possible. Our appreciation for the words of God grew exponentially: "Now the Lord is the Spirit, and where the Spirit of the Lord is, there is freedom" (2 Cor. 3:17).

LEADING WITH A WHISPER

In God's amazing timing David and I one day had lunch with our friend and an executive leader in the US Assemblies of God, George Wood, PhD. He had strongly encouraged my doctoral studies and was interested in this new ministry, Project Rescue. But during that lunch, he had something else on his mind.

"Beth, I'm concerned about the women ministering in our movement," he said. "We have had female ministers and ordination for them since the early years of the Assemblies of God. There are now many more open doors for women in secular America. But the percentage of ordained female ministers in our movement has been declining. Why do you think that is? What can we do to change that direction and encourage them?"

What a welcome question and concern coming from an executive leader! That brainstorming session at a diner with George Wood was soon followed by an official proposal from General Superintendent Thomas Trask and the executive leadership team for the National Task Force for Women in Ministry. Its sole mandate at the time was to propose, plan, and implement the very first Assemblies of God National Conference for Women in Ministry. The task force included Rev. Joyce Bridges; Billie Davis, EdD; Deborah Gill, PhD; Rev. Alicia Chole; Rev. Judy Rachels; Carolyn Tennant, PhD; and Rev. Lillian Sparks. I was appointed to serve as chair. As I began to know, pray with, and work with these women, I discovered if you wanted a dream team of strong, godly, and competent women to break ground with, this was that team.

Eighteen months later, in early 2001 the first National Conference for Women in Ministry convened in Springfield, Missouri. Themed "The Spirit of the Lord Is upon Me," 1,500 female ministers representing three generations came together with excitement to be encouraged, affirmed, validated, and freshly

A Voice for God's Daughters

anointed for ministry. Now, if you put that many Pentecostal women in one place at one time, you'll have your hands full as a leader! The sisters came ready to preach, prophesy, and bring spiritual words.

And the executive leaders of the Assemblies of God, who had invited me to take this assignment, were sitting on the front row, smiling widely. I could be wrong, but it felt like those wise smiles were saying, "Have at it, Beth. This one's yours!" Our task force believed God ordained that first conference for His called daughters. This was His time for female ministers of all ages to step up in unity to be affirmed, encouraged, and boldly released into His purposes for their lives. Both male and female leaders believed the church would become stronger and more effective in fulfilling God's mission locally and globally in the years ahead because of it, and our executive leaders, whom I deeply respected, had thrown the door open wide. We seized the moment.

At the end of the conference a young woman who was studying for a graduate degree at a secular university came to me privately.

"Beth, the only model I have had in my lifetime for strong women in leadership has been a secular, feminist one," she said. "As a Jesus follower I've been uneasy with the militance of that. But this conference has given me a whole new model of competent, professional, strong female leaders that reflect the spirit of Jesus. I can do that! You have given me hope."

I will always be grateful to George Wood for believing biblically, theologically, and soundly in practice that God does indeed call and anoint women for service. He was a pivotal leader in our movement, paving an organizational way forward for future generations of women called of God. One day, we will all celebrate what God has done together in heaven.

In ten years, the National Task Force for Women in Ministry planned and convened several national and regional conferences for female ministers of all ages. One of the greatest joys of those years was walking and working with multigifted, like-minded women of God on the task force and with hundreds of other female leaders from across America as well. They in turn have encouraged, equipped, and strengthened the hands of thousands of other female ministers in their circles of spiritual influence in the United States and overseas.

As David and I had been witnessing in the church across Southern Asia, God was raising up an army of called, qualified women here in America. Simultaneously, we had the opportunity to connect with male church leaders on both sides of the world. God was speaking to many of them too, about His call on their wives. With a little help from the Lord and my husband they began to realize it was their responsibility to affirm His call, bless, and release their wives to also do the work of the Lord.

Over those years, there were strategic opportunities for me to recommend younger female ministers on whom one could see God's powerful hand. At the beginning of the National Task Force for Women in Ministry, friends who were national church leaders acknowledged they knew very few female ministers that they might suggest for national platform ministry. Now, that was an oversight and opportunity! Leaders can share platforms and recommend guest preachers, speakers, missionaries, and evangelists only if they know them, or at least know their names and that they have a strong recommendation from someone else respected in ministry.

Many times, when someone is promoted or given opportunities, I've heard onlookers say, "Well, it's all about who you know!" One day, I started thinking about that statement. Opportunities or positions of any kind can't really be about who we *don't* know, can they? People (including Christian leaders) naturally recommend people they know.

If we serve in ministry and leadership, we have the privilege and responsibility to facilitate the ministry of others in the body of Christ. One of the greatest gifts we can give is to commend others for ministry—women and men. Whether God gives us the privilege of a platform in a small group, on a podcast, on the street, or in a large church, we can share it, even if only for five minutes. If God opens a door for us personally, let's take someone younger with us as we walk through it. When we receive an invitation we cannot accept (or are not qualified to accept!), let's generously recommend other female ministers who are qualified and Spirit empowered instead.

The apostle Paul was a great role model in that regard. He commended to others both male and female colaborers who served the early church well. (See Acts 15:22; 16:14, 34; 18:1; 19:1; 20:4; 21:8, 16; 27:3; Philippians 2:25; Romans 16:1–3; 2 Timothy 4:19; and many others.) For the sake of building God's kingdom and church in the world, let's strategically do the same.

It is a testimony to the love of God and the power of the gospel itself that those things are transformative for women who call upon His name in faith—whether they are bound in sexual slavery or in churches around the world. When women have the opportunity to meet and receive Jesus, He saves them from sin and shame, heals broken hearts, and restores broken lives. Women of all ages who seek Him can be empowered by His Spirit and the gifts He has given them to participate in His redemptive mission to others! Like Mary Magdalene and the

Samaritan woman at the well, women who encounter Jesus go from being among those who desperately need new life to being those who become vibrant voices to others, sharing about Jesus, the only giver of new life.

The global community of faith is privileged to carry this good news to women and girls of the world. Whether in a church in Richmond, Virginia, or a red-light district in Southern Asia, our Father celebrates every prodigal daughter who's been set free by His Son to become a strong, courageous woman of faith. Heaven rejoices, and so do we!

Several years ago a speech professor at a Christian university invited me to speak to his class about how I personally prepare sermons. During the presentation, a young male student and his girlfriend sitting in the very back of the room caught my attention. The man's body language and attitude were openly disrespectful.

At the end of my presentation the professor welcomed students to ask questions. The young man pushed back his chair and was the first to respond.

"How can you defend being a woman in the pulpit?" he asked.

I was a little taken aback, not expecting to hear that particular question there. But in a quiet voice I simply said the first thing that came to my mind: "Quite honestly, I have never felt the need to defend my obedience to God." The young man was silent. But he had inadvertently helped clear the air and open the door for our moving on to some excellent questions from other students.

REFLECTIONS ON WOMEN IN MINISTRY

Walking and working with young female ministers in the United States, Europe, and Southern Asia have been a passion

A Voice for God's Daughters

and privilege of my journey for several decades. That journey has provided rich opportunities to observe, reflect, and go back to Scripture again and again regarding God's calling upon women and girls and how we navigate that call both within the church and in our larger world. I'd like to share a few observations for your personal reflection.

1. Divergent views on women in ministry are still with us throughout the body of Christ, and I suspect they always will be until we all go to heaven. Whether they are found in denominations, local churches, or families, those views can be divisive, disheartening, and sometimes hurtful. In the spirit of humility it's important to remember that the most eloquent, well-argued theological views we hear (or voice) are still human. Scripture, from beginning to end, shows us plainly it is God who knows and calls anyone He wills by name—whether we look more like Deborah or David. The sovereign God appoints people, pours out His anointing oil on sons and daughters, and faithfully makes a way for those on whom He places His hand. There is no better waymaker or door opener than Him!

We can respectfully agree or disagree with one another's views on women in ministry, but I am personally accountable to live out my life to please the One who asks in a still, small voice, "Beth, will you still follow Me?" And after all the decades of debate about women in ministry have fallen silent, my answer will remain, "Yes, Lord, I will follow You."

Admittedly, at times that yes came with some tears. Other times, it came with a shout of excitement. But let's move on, my friend. If God has laid His hand on us for His kingdom mission in this strategic day of harvest, let's be about our Father's business. (And if you are a Pentecostal theologian who is called and gifted by God to be a voice for His daughters in ministry, don't let me slow you down!)

2. For serving in ministry or church leadership it's critical that

you are confident in your identity in Christ—not your identity as someone's mother, someone's daughter, someone's wife or sister, or someone's pastor or professor. Many may know me as "David Grant's wife," which I am, and which I love being. But that's not where my peace and confidence are when people's words or Satan's lies hit me head-on. Like the apostle Paul, who said, "For to me, to live is Christ" (Phil. 1:21), our strong foundation is knowing who we are in Him!

3. Every male leader, pastor, evangelist, and teacher who discerns the call of God on women and girls and advocates for them on their journeys is a gift, like my pastor Ervin Mason when I was fifteen. They are colaborers and brothers in Christ. It's a privilege to work shoulder to shoulder with gifted, godly male colleagues and to walk out the mission of God together.

We celebrate the victories won together. But when we find ourselves in tough spots as leaders, I also want my male colleagues to know that when they pass the ball to me, they can trust me not to drop it. We are not here to do the will of God in spite of each other; we do it in relationship with each other. My sentiments are captured by what the great missionary general Charles Greenaway once said: "I'll do everything I can to help you. But if I can't help you, I sure won't hurt you!" I seriously question whether men and women in the body of Christ can work together in spiritual leadership as well as God intends if we are actively or even subconsciously competing with each other.

As we value being one in Christ and intentionally discern the image of God and His gifts in one another, female and male leadership teams in the body of Christ have the capacity and opportunities to set a higher bar for collaboration in a secular world marked by competitiveness, dismissiveness, stereotypical thinking, and abuses of power. Our mandate as individual believers is to be like Jesus. But leaders and leadership teams in the body of Christ are called to look like Jesus too.

A Voice for God's Daughters

4. From a New Testament perspective, I cannot make a case for ministry being a right for anyone—male or female. Every disciple's journey with Jesus, since the time He was on earth, began with an invitation to literally sacrifice their life: "Whoever wants to be my disciple must deny themselves and take up their cross daily and follow me. For whoever wants to save their life will lose it, but whoever loses their life for me will save it" (Luke 9:23–24). God's call to serve in ministry or leadership is a holy, humbling call and a privilege. It in no way modifies the first and most important call of Jesus: to give ourselves as living sacrifices and to take up His cross. That's not "rights" language. (See "The Best Is Yet to Come: Why Credentialed Women Ministers Matter to the Assemblies of God" by George O. Wood, James T. Bradford, and Beth Grant.[1])

In one of the most sobering passages in the New Testament, Paul exhorts the Philippian believers, both male and female:

> In your relationships with one another, have the same mindset as Christ Jesus: Who, being in very nature God, did not consider equality with God something to be used to his own advantage; rather, he made himself nothing by taking the very nature of a servant, being made in human likeness. And being found in appearance as a man, he humbled himself by becoming obedient to death—even death on a cross!
>
> —PHILIPPIANS 2:5–8

The more closely our personal journeys with Jesus reflect His Philippians 2 example, I pray the more our private and denominational conversations about women and men in ministry will look and sound like Him too.

5. Some days, people bless and affirm us. I'm grateful to God and them for those times. And other days, people don't. In all

LEADING WITH A WHISPER

cases we can continue to walk in God's truth, guard our hearts from bitterness, and serve Him however He leads. People cannot cancel God's call, nor can they disqualify us from ministry. But unhealed hurts, resentments, and bitterness that are allowed to take root in our lives can. To do long-term ministry with strength and spiritual health, David and I came to a point when we knew we had to choose forgiveness as a daily spiritual discipline rather than as a case-by-case decision that depended on the circumstances. During very difficult challenges in our leadership over several years, we determined that nothing anyone has done to us or said about us is worth missing what God has for us to fulfill over a lifetime of serving Him. Although it's not easy or natural, we discovered we can lean in to the grace of God and continue to forgive like Jesus daily.

To be clear, this does not indicate we can trust some of those individuals again or should ever put ourselves in harm's way. No. But we can choose to forgive in prayer before God and receive healing and the freedom to move on with Jesus, whether we ever receive an apology from those individuals or not.

6. Positions for ministry and leadership come and go. Serve well wherever you find yourself, but hold positions lightly. We fill them, but we do not own them. God's call, His passion, and the gifts He gives are what remain fresh from season to season.

7. Never apologize for your God-given strengths and gifts. Used with grace and generously dedicated to God, they will enable you to walk out His sovereign call with dignity, courage, and victory—all for His glory. The best case for having women in ministry is ultimately the well-lived, Spirit-anointed lives and ministries of countless women in the multicultural church around the world. The fact that God continues to call and pour out His Spirit on daughters who sacrificially obey Him cannot be dismissed.

This is not an American phenomenon. As was true in the

A Voice for God's Daughters

early decades of the Assemblies of God a century ago, single and widowed women can be found today serving missionally in some of the most difficult, demonized places in the world. They inspire and challenge me! Why would any woman choose a dangerous, sacrificial journey far from family and home that may cost her everything—including the opportunities for marriage, remarriage, and children—or possibly even cost her life? No, my friend, she's not doing that because she's ambitious. She's doing it because she's been called by God and sent on His redeeming mission to the ends of the earth.

LISA'S STORY

My friend and pioneering colleague Lisa Russi is one such called, courageous woman. Here is her story in her own words:

> God called me to the mission field at nine years old in an old airport hangar that the Indiana AG campground called "the Tabernacle." He confirmed this call at sixteen when I prayed, "Lord, I will do whatever You want, and I'll go wherever You want me to go." I remember telling the two most important women in my life: my mother and my grandmother. My grandmother, a pillar of faith and a major support in my life, smiled and said she already knew.
>
> The next step for me was to attend Evangel University in Springfield, Missouri. There, I studied social work while also taking missions courses as electives. When Beth spoke in chapel, I knew I wanted to take her course and learn more about her work in Southern Asia. Growing up, I tried to talk to every missionary that came to my church. They were almost always married men, and their wives were either not present or busy with their children. Despite growing up

103

within the Assemblies of God, Beth was the first female missionary I had a chance to learn from.

One month after graduation, I was in Bangladesh volunteering in a children's home. I quickly moved into leadership and responsibility roles in the children's home, as well as within the national church. Toward the end of my three-year term, I was asked to travel to the southern border to help with a local church ministry for six weeks. There, I met a local woman ministering to women in a brothel. She invited me to a brothel village on the water at the jungle's edge.

When we arrived by boat, the women immediately invited us to tea. Each of them took turns telling their stories. Most women were young widows who were dropped off at the brothel or sold by their in-laws after their husbands tragically died. However, sitting just to my left was a very young girl, around twelve or thirteen, who was holding a baby. When it was her turn to speak, she told me she was born in that brothel village and forced into prostitution at five years of age. The little baby she was holding wasn't her brother, as I had guessed, but her child. She was nearly the same age as my youngest sister, and I kept saying to the Lord, "She could be my sister!"

As we left, I felt the Holy Spirit say, "This is your sister, and so is every woman and child in this situation. And if your sister was in this situation, what would you do to help her?"

I left Southern Asia a few weeks later certain of my call. I returned after three years with a graduate degree and, in partnership with Project Rescue and the national church, started a home for the girls who had been born in brothels. Once a local leader emerged in Bangladesh, God called me to France to pioneer a similar work with the national church for survivors of human trafficking. Project Rescue was expanding its network to Europe, so I once again partnered with them to start Perles de Prix in France. Currently, with coleader Joy Krajicek we have started ministries in four cities through local churches.

Looking back on my life, I realize God prepared me from birth for this call. My grandmother, an orphan forced into child labor and a survivor of bride kidnapping, had a life full of suffering before she found Christ. Yet the woman I knew was full of joy, peace, and love. She modeled to me from an early age the fact that Christ is the key to transformation in the face of horrific trauma. I am privileged to take this message to my sisters around the world.

Future Generations of Leaders

To advocate for God's daughters means advocating for God's daughters for generations to come. It's advocating for hidden women who, because of their cultures, will most likely have to hear the good news from a woman. Many women in barren places around the world are crying out to a God they do not know to help them in their terror and distress. Who will go to them? From the beginning of the Assemblies of God, strong, fearless young women like Lisa have worked as pioneers on the edge of vast darkness and brought the One who is light—again and again and again!

Women friends who are leaders in other denominations remind me at times how blessed we are as women in the Assemblies of God to have the option to be credentialed ministers. No, we are not perfect, for sure. But we are blessed. The church was instituted by God, but it is made up of people like us who are still human. But with God's help—and courageous, wise male and female advocates throughout our history until now—women have become an integral part of our ministry family and an increasingly normalized part of AG leadership.

Note, in 1998 when George Wood expressed concern to me about the low numbers of women choosing to take ministerial credentials in the Assemblies of God, they were at least 15 percent of the total credentialed ministry family.[2] As of today, twenty-seven years later, credentialed women now represent roughly 30 percent of total ministers.[3] As I write, there are 11,046 credentialed female ministers in the US Assemblies of God and more than 700 across America who serve as Assemblies of God lead pastors.[4] And God faithfully keeps pouring out His Spirit on hungry sons and daughters around the world—just as He promised He would do through the prophet Joel:

> I will pour out my Spirit on all people. Your sons and daughters will prophesy, your old men will dream dreams, your young men will see visions. Even on my servants, both men and women, I will pour out my Spirit in those days.
>
> —JOEL 2:28–29

QUESTIONS FOR REFLECTION

1. As a follower of Jesus how do you recognize and encourage God's calling in the lives of young girls and women within your sphere of influence? Prayerfully reflect on ways you can be more intentional in equipping them to fulfill their God-given purposes. As a leader how can you strategically

A Voice for God's Daughters

integrate this into your personal ministry or your church's mission?

2. If you are a woman called by God, how do you navigate differing opinions about your calling? What practical strategies have helped you stay grounded and effective in walking out God's call? Whether you are male or female, how do you support and encourage other women and girls on whom you sense God's call?

3. I do not know a woman of God who has not faced discouragement or conflicting responses to her calling because of her gender. If God Himself did not make ministry or calling a gender issue, how can we avoid falling into that trap ourselves? What practical steps can we take to maintain a faith-filled and courageous perspective, both during tough times and in seasons of great victory?

4. I see great potential for men and women leaders to work side by side in the church and in God's global mission. What are some ways leaders can set a higher bar for successful collaboration for the sake of the kingdom? Identify some biblical principles that can inform how women and men work together in ministry, applying a standard that sets us apart from both secular and traditional religious norms.

From the left: Anita Koeshall, PhD; me; Deborah Gill, PhD; Melody Palm, PsyD; and Ava Oleson, DMin—women leaders and advocate friends who have served for decades in missions, theological education, and psychology and are strong voices for women in leadership and ministry

A promotional piece for our Conversations 10 event

Chapter 10

A Seat at the Table

DAVID AND I were in Kansas City, Missouri, in 2001 to participate in an Assemblies of God General Council. One evening, Pastor Jim Cymbala of The Brooklyn Tabernacle preached a powerful, convicting sermon specifically for ministers and leaders. At the end of it, along with hundreds of others I found a place near the altar to pray and respond.

That night, God spoke clearly to me through my tears. "Beth, I am asking you to be willing to be more visible, more public, and a voice for Me. Are you willing to sacrifice more of your privacy, to step out in faith beyond your preferred supportive role with David, and to be available to Me?"

I was broken. And because I felt the weight and implications of God's question, my response was slow in coming.

"Lord, You know I will give You anything—time, finances—I'll go anywhere, no problem," I finally said. *But to become more public and visible?* With my face on the floor sometime later when the tears were done, I quietly laid it down.

"Lord, I'll be willing. And I will be a voice. *But if You really want me to be a voice, You must give me a voice.* If You do, I'll go where You open the door and try to say what You want me to say in faith and in Your power."

No one knew about that encounter with God, including my husband. But I sensed that the One whose preparation is impeccable was bringing me into a different season of saying yes to Jesus.

Front-row seats to history, whether in a denomination, government, ministry, or theater, may come with some honor. But they always have a price. (If you don't believe me, ask Queen Esther.)

That's why in 2009 when the Assemblies of God was electing the first female executive presbyter in its ninety-five-year history to serve on its governing board, I was thrilled it was happening. But I stayed quiet about it in public. Marrying David had come with a measure of visibility, and serving with the National Task Force for Women in Ministry naturally heightened that visibility. But my prayer had always been, "Lord, I want to be where You want me to be with all my heart. But I don't want to be anywhere You have not chosen for me. Please direct my steps in this, and make Your will clear."

It was a historic moment for the Assemblies of God USA when the first woman executive presbyter was elected to serve on behalf of an army of eight thousand credentialed female ministers. It was humbling to hear that woman would be me. I stood and looked out at the faces of hundreds of women who were friends and colleagues in ministry with tears filling my eyes. This moment was theirs. It reflected their sacrificial, courageous service to God all over the world. And God gave me peace to serve, sensing that this somehow was His doing.

And God bless my husband! He enthusiastically walked with me every step of the way. That afternoon, he was so happy to escort me to the platform. Afterward as he escorted me out to begin serving at this new table of leadership, I managed a whisper. "David Grant, you brought me to this party. But don't you ever forget—I'm going home with you!"

A Seat at the Table

That moment began fourteen years of service with a seat at the table of the Executive Presbytery in the Assemblies of God. This was and is my home church, and I care deeply about it. I've been passionate about the extent to which we stay focused on the global mission our founders committed themselves to in 1914. And over the years of working in some very dark places, I learned firsthand why Jesus told His newly commissioned disciples in the Book of Acts not to leave the Upper Room until they received His Spirit's power to "go into all the world" (Acts 1:4–5, paraphrased; Mark 16:15). He knew the Great Commission was impossible without His supernatural power. And I knew it was in God's plan that women and men be fully engaged together and integrated into the mission through this church and in the power of Pentecost.

So I began serving in the presbytery, with a seat at the table alongside my male colleagues. A few years later it was very exciting when some new female colleagues were elected to join the executive leadership table as well.

From the first meeting, I was struck by the articulate voices within the Executive Presbytery. There was the deep, resonant voice of Pastor Dan Betzer, most famous for his *Revivaltime* national radio career and the beloved *Dan and Louie* children's Bible stories. He did not speak often, but when he did, it was like Moses coming down off the mountain with the Ten Commandments!

Then, there was Pastor J. Don George from Dallas. He was so eloquent that if the "distinguished senator from Texas" spoke, it was over. The chairman and general superintendent, George Wood, was a brilliant lawyer, theologian, and exceptional preacher. They were just three of an impressive board of nationally and internationally known speakers.

111

And suddenly, there was Beth. That first meeting, I listened and privately asked God, "Are You sure about this, Lord? What can I bring to this table?"

My voice had never been very strong. And after David and I married, the years of constant international travel with changing climates and bouts of laryngitis had left my voice even weaker. Over time it became more and more unreliable. Often, whether speaking publicly in restaurants or churches or talking privately to our girls, I had to work hard to be heard beyond a whisper. Rebecca and Jennifer even had a name for it when they were in trouble: It was "Mom's power whisper."

Now here I was at a large, generous boardroom table surrounded by men, and a few of them were already having difficulties with their hearing. George Wood (and later his successor, Rev. Doug Clay) and the staff began to place microphones near me in board meetings to help everyone hear my voice. Over time, staff would suddenly show up with a mic if I stepped up to speak publicly. The team could not have been more gracious and helpful.

No one knew that God had spoken to me at that Kansas City altar and asked me to be willing to be a voice for Him—and I sure wasn't going to tell them! With God and some great tech help, sometimes when I would speak at public meetings, my voice grew stronger. But sitting at a long board table, making myself heard was always an effort.

I was a missionary-educator and the only one at the table who had never served as a pastor or district leader in the Assemblies of God USA. So Robert's Rules of order, how to draft a formal resolution, and protocols for ministerial discipline were largely foreign to me. (On the other hand, I could tell them a few things about ministry for Jesus in a red-light district.)

Since this was the first opportunity to have a woman on any committee, I became that woman and attended a lot of committee meetings. I ended up smiling a lot, listening in overdrive, and

A Seat at the Table

starting a steep learning curve. I do love to learn, so saying, "Help me understand," served me well. Thankfully, there were humorous moments when all us male and female leaders were learning how to do this side by side, together.

- The new Under Forty representative, Pastor Bryan Jarrett, and I waded into our new Executive Presbytery roles together. Sometimes, concerning agenda items would be brought to the table and discussed as if there was no solution. And we both would be thinking, "There is an obvious solution here. Why isn't anyone mentioning that?" So a few meetings in I raised my hand and suggested a possible step forward on one of those items. There was silence. Men looked awkwardly at each other. The chair asked, "Would anyone care to speak to that?" Again, there was silence. (I think men are more comfortable with few words and letting something die on the table in silence, with no kind word to soften the blow, than women are.)

  Finally, the chair said simply, "OK, moving on." From that moment, I was grateful to God there was a lot more to what I could bring to the table than one naive idea.

  Later, I found out there was a story behind that particular issue that everyone else in the meeting was aware of, but which had not been documented. (There always is, and honestly, I'm not sure anyone wanted a solution to that one.) Later, I remembered what my best coach advised me when I was elected to serve as an executive presbyter: "Don't say anything for a year." Too late!

- A seat at the table requires participating in serious, complex discussions. In the middle of one of those discussions, the chair called for a coffee break. Afterward, we resumed, and I assumed we'd continue the important discussion where we had left off. But instead, the vote was called, and it was pretty unanimous. Hmm. After several similar incidents, I began to realize the conversation about the issue apparently continued and was concluded in the men's restroom over the break—most likely with almost no words. Obviously, they had a quorum, since only one of us was missing.

- We board members were learning there's more to working together as men and women in leadership than remembering not to call the women *guys*. That's one of the things they had to learn too, but that was by far the easiest part.

It was a lot of work—but it was and is well worth it! Over these years, I've watched male and female board members who were genuinely committed to growth learn how to serve well together. We've learned to value one another in our different God-given gifts. And while I wasn't thrilled with my voice, nor was I there to sound like anyone else at the table. I would have been foolish to try to do that.

The number of female leaders serving at board and governance tables has grown greatly across our denomination since that time. David and I celebrate the progress that has been made in our church and mission. God-called, competent, anointed women and men ministering shoulder to shoulder is no longer an exception but a growing norm. The global task of executing God's mission and urgently bringing in the harvest in these prophetic days deserves and demands our best—male and female leaders united in their God-given tasks, strengths, skills, and spiritual gifts.

There are always weighty aspects to having a seat at the table. Board members know difficult things that you would be happier not to know. You only know certain things because you bear the responsibility to pray over and discuss them and then make a decision as a body. And heavy decisions have sobering implications.

Many times, I left the table with a very heavy heart, grieving over situations and people within the family of faith for which there were no easy answers. I'm so grateful for the many executive church leaders across our nation who believe in Spirit-led intercession at board tables and in church services, leaders who are not ashamed to cry out to God for His help. At our collective best we still are not enough to take care of all God's business. But He hears the cries of those who know they are desperate for Him and call upon His name—including leaders who serve at tables of governance.

Sometimes people ask me what it's like to serve on an executive governance board. When they do, I remember a quote from a pilot who flew very long international flights and was asked what his job was like. The pilot responded, "Thousands of hours of boredom and moments of sheer terror!"

Now, that may be a bit of an exaggeration in describing

service on Christian executive boards. But hours of poring over reports and discussing agenda items, protocol, and business are never exciting for any board—Christian or not. But those hours of routine can be punctuated by moments when you suddenly realize what someone just said or recommended has stunning missional implications. If board members are zoned out, distracted by social media, or taking a break, decisions can be made or resolutions passed about which people will later say, "*How in the world did that ever happen?*" Most likely *that* happened in the middle of hours of routine business proceedings.

A seat at an executive board table comes with a price and a responsibility. I personally felt that if I was not fully present—mentally, spiritually, and with my voice ready—for those potential few "moments of sheer terror," I would have wasted my seat at the table. I could have failed to serve God and His church. My prayer was that God would help me steward my seat and my voice well.

There have been moments when God nudged me by His Spirit to speak from my seat at a table. When that has happened, I generally paused to see if those words would come from someone else first. If so, it was a quiet confirmation, and my voice wasn't needed. But if not, and this sense from God grew stronger, I've learned to trust Him and speak. He is always faithful. And in some of those moments, God wonderfully confirmed His guidance when board members collectively sensed, "This seems good to the Holy Spirit and to us."

After several years of serving on the Executive Presbytery, I went to see a voice specialist. She diagnosed me with spasmodic dysphonia, a disorder in which the vocal cords spasm and can

A Seat at the Table

cause breaking in the voice every few sentences. The voice may sound strained and be reduced to a whisper. It is untreatable.

There was actually some relief to know there was a medical cause for what I'd been experiencing more frequently over the years, a reason why I couldn't trust my voice. But the diagnosis did something else: It reminded me I had never taken one step on the ministry journey God called me to because I could trust my voice or any other one natural gift. I dared to step into God's calling as He led me because I really did trust Him.

Whatever good has come in ministry and missions through my life has flowed from the hand of a compassionate, faithful God. He anointed me by His Spirit for His good purposes. And He asked me in a later season of my life to be available to be a voice. To this day, that's a bit of a mystery to me. But regardless of our limitations, God's power to do more than anything we can think of or even imagine has not changed. Will we remain available to Him in our weakness?

Since that time, when God opens a door for me and it's time to minister, His voice through my voice is strong. Sometimes all I have is a whisper. But when the Spirit of the Lord anoints, there's fire in that whisper. No vocal disorder, or any other human frailty, can put out the Spirit's fire that burns in our souls.

STEWARDING GOD'S GIFT OF VOICE

Here are a few of the things I've learned along the way about this.

1. Save your voice.

If we speak to everything, our voices are no longer heard, whether with a husband, child, board table, church, or on social media. Don't waste your gift of voice on unworthy causes—to demean, dishonor, demonize, shame, or tear down people God loves. You only have one voice. Save it for words, messages, and moments that matter.

2. Use your voice.

Use your gift of voice wisely to speak God's truth with compassion and clarity. Become known for consistently speaking words that are gracious, encouraging, redeeming, healing, affirming, and liberating. Speak words of truth that are not only aligned with God's Word but also aligned with His Spirit. He anoints His people with words of exhortation, wisdom, knowledge, discernment, prophecy, and repentance. When it's God's moment, speak with courage and in His authority.

3. Protect your voice.

There are righteous and unrighteous causes in our world. As a minister and leader, pick your battles well. Not every good battle is ours to fight personally. If we use our voices, energy, and goodwill for every battle that comes along, we can be distracted and unprepared for the most strategic battles God has personally called us to take on.

4. Get His Word in your voice.

Read it aloud in your quiet time with God so it becomes more than words on a page. The more we read important passages and promises aloud, the more they will go beyond our intellects to grow in our spirits and souls. The passages will come alive and be quickened in our voices as we share—whether one-on-one in a coffee shop, with others in a small group, to many from a traditional platform, or from a seat at the executive board table.

STEWARDING A SEAT AT THE TABLE

1. Approach each new table assignment recognizing that, in most cases, while your arrival may be a new day for you personally, it is not a new day for that table. History, relationships, and complex matters of business are already in play—and

A Seat at the Table

have been for years sometimes. The only way to understand the context for agenda items beyond what you can see on paper is to become very observant and a good listener.

2. Approach the table as a learner with good questions, not as the person who has the answers. People who serve well and long on boards continue to ask the best questions. Thoughtful questions can lead a team to thoughtful answers. For example, what is the important question you wonder why no one is asking? In time, you'll gain wisdom into what questions do need to be asked and which questions are best to let go unasked.

3. Do your homework. It's hard to engage and track well on a board if we're reading lengthy documents for the first time as business quickly proceeds.

4. Pray for discernment, especially if the board is responsible to God's church, mission, or leadership. Sometimes the stated agenda is not as important as an underlying agenda. When you sense that, pray for wisdom and God's leading. Some things are best ignored, and silence is wisdom. Other times, look to a wise veteran. How is that person responding?

5. Come to the table aware and practicing God's presence—especially when weighty matters are on the agenda and board members are not unified around them. There have been times I've experienced God using board members to bring a word of wisdom, knowledge, or discernment,

119

LEADING WITH A WHISPER

and even prophetic words. God can do more in moments by His Spirit and gifts through spiritually sensitive board members than we can do on our own in months.

6. Research has documented that women tend to use more words than men do to say the same thing.[1] I hadn't thought of myself as wordy until I sat on the Executive Presbytery. Maybe I was, and that really made me aware of it. Male colleagues at the table had an impressive way of communicating concisely with very few words. So when I joined, I immediately began to try to tighten up my words. When I felt speaking to a matter was important, I'd make a quick note to myself to make it more concise before I spoke.

7. Remember, don't take yourself too seriously. We need to be able to laugh at ourselves when we don't get it right.

8. Lastly, when it comes to tables, be remembered for your wisdom, not for your gender.

SERVING AT TABLES

From the first times I was invited to serve on the board of a Christian institution or denomination, I've often thought about the time Jesus also sat at a table near the end of His life.

It was just before the Passover Festival. Jesus knew that the hour had come for him to leave this world and go to the Father. Having loved his own who were in the world, he loved them to the end.

The evening meal was in progress, and the devil had

A Seat at the Table

already prompted Judas, the son of Simon Iscariot, to betray Jesus. Jesus knew that the Father had put all things under his power, and that he had come from God and was returning to God; so he got up from the meal, took off his outer clothing, and wrapped a towel around his waist. After that, he poured water into a basin and began to wash his disciples' feet, drying them with the towel that was wrapped around him.

He came to Simon Peter, who said to him, "Lord, are you going to wash my feet?"

Jesus replied, "You do not realize now what I am doing, but later you will understand."

"No," said Peter, "you shall never wash my feet."

Jesus answered, "Unless I wash you, you have no part with me."

"Then, Lord," Simon Peter replied, "not just my feet but my hands and my head as well!"

Jesus answered, "Those who have had a bath need only to wash their feet; their whole body is clean. And you are clean, though not every one of you." For he knew who was going to betray him, and that was why he said not every one was clean.

When he had finished washing their feet, he put on his clothes and returned to his place. "Do you understand what I have done for you?" he asked them. "You call me 'Teacher' and 'Lord,' and rightly so, for that is what I am. Now that I, your Lord and Teacher, have washed your feet, you also should wash one another's feet. I have set you an example that you should do as I have done for you. Very truly I tell you, no servant is greater than his master, nor is a messenger greater than the one who sent him. Now that you know these things, you will be blessed if you do them."

—JOHN 13:1–17

LEADING WITH A WHISPER

There is no way for me to take up the towel and wash feet as Jesus commanded His disciples without humbling myself and being willing to serve others. I've had good church leaders in very hierarchical cultures tell me, "But Beth, you don't understand. That's harder in our culture than it is for you as an American. We have servants in our culture; we *know* what being a servant looks like. And that's very hard for our leaders to do." Yes, humbly taking up the towel like Jesus is very hard in hierarchical cultures.

But the more I've grappled with that passage from the perspective of our more egalitarian Western cultures, I believe we have just as much difficulty taking up the towel as others, but for different reasons. We want everything in life ideally to be equal, even in sacrifice and so-called serving. So we do interesting things with Jesus' instruction for us to take up the towel. We're happy to do so—as long as our colleagues in leadership or in the church carry their comparable end of the load too. Let's not get carried away in serving if someone else on our ministry team is not doing as much to serve as we are! To put it in our more egalitarian framework, said or unsaid, the thinking may be, "I'll wash your feet, but I expect you to wash mine too." So even though I'm willing to participate in the privilege of serving in leadership, I want to make sure we're all similarly willing to do our part.

When the Son of God physically stooped down to pick up a common towel, knelt, and washed His very human disciples' feet, He challenged our pride as disciples in any time and any culture. For men and women who follow Jesus in any culture in the world this passage presents a challenge.

So has there ever been a way for disciples to take up the towel in ministry and leadership in the spirit of Jesus without being willing to serve the many and be used by a few? In my American culture there's a fear of, or even a deep-seated aversion to, being used or having someone take advantage of us. I've had colleagues

122

A Seat at the Table

warn me about someone possibly "using me." But since David and I have worked in cultures where servants are common, valued, and important to life and community, the more I've observed the obvious: *Good servants are always used.* They are chosen. They are the most available, with few conditions, and they consistently serve well. That's the point. That's the role of good servants.

Over the course of my life I've been deeply inspired by leaders who serve with excellence and in the spirit of Jesus. They are consistently welcomed to minister, lead, and serve at tables of governance over time. God Himself uses good servants and servant leaders. And so do a few people who have their own agendas.

But Jesus' example at the table with His disciples challenges me (and maybe you!) to this day. Jesus washed the feet of the one who was literally going to betray Him. Judas stayed put and got a good foot washing from the Son of God. But more importantly Jesus stooped down and washed the feet of eleven disciples who loved Him, would live their lives for Him, and even *give* their lives for Him. They slipped away from the table that night having had a very discomfortable experience with their Master that likely challenged and reframed the way they viewed following Him and serving others for the rest of their lives.

When God gives us a seat at the table, let's never forget the towel.

QUESTIONS FOR REFLECTION

1. Ministering out of God's calling and our spiritual and physical strengths is a joy and privilege. But sometimes God calls us to serve from a place of weakness or where we feel unqualified. Reflect on times when you obeyed Him despite feeling weak. How was His strength made perfect and His power and glory made more apparent in that situation?

LEADING WITH A WHISPER

2. Reflect on a time while serving at a table of leadership or governance when, like the international pilot, you felt a moment of sheer terror. What did you learn from that experience? What advice would you give to someone who is serving in church leadership for the first time?

3. In the section "Stewarding God's Gift of Voice" what advice stood out to you the most in your current stage of life and ministry? Why? Can you find any Bible verses that encourage you to steward your voice and recognize the importance of this gift?

4. In this chapter I talk about serving in leadership (at tables of governance) in the church and about how Jesus set an example of servant leadership by taking up the towel and washing His disciples' feet. As people grow in leadership and influence, do you think it becomes harder to stay humble and serve like Jesus? Why, or why not? What have you learned from those in leadership who serve with both Christlike humility and spiritual authority?

My heart was full of gratitude to God and my fellow ministers at the 2009 General Council when I was given the privilege of serving as the first female executive presbyter.

Courtesy of the Assemblies of God

The 2011 elected body of executive presbyters

It has been a joy and privilege to serve with excellent, competent, and called women leaders at the Executive Presbytery table: (from left) Melissa Alfaro, PhD, formerly the Under Forty representative, now serves as the executive presbyter representing credentialed women, and Rev. Donna Barrett serves as General Secretary. (Rev. Maricela Hernández is absent from the photo but also serves as a regional executive presbyter.)

Chapter 11

No Turning Back (Reprise)

FROM THE TIME David and I married and went to Southern Asia together, we had an unspoken but shared awareness: Our yes to take Jesus into certain nations and very spiritually challenging places where injustice ruled could have costs. Only God knew what they would be, but we knew some of the possibilities.

So we lived by praying and trusting God for wisdom literally to navigate the journey. But we also prayed for courage to live in faith and to be fully engaged in what God had clearly called His people to do. Planting churches, establishing training schools, biblically empowering women, and working through Project Rescue with sexually exploited women and children were all pursued in collaboration with our national church leaders and friends. They were called men and women of God who took great steps of faith on behalf of the gospel in their own lands, and they were very familiar with their local contexts and the cost of following Jesus; they lived with a passion to share God's love. His work was in good hands.

Being foreigners who spoke in churches and worked in areas controlled by organized crime, we were aware of growing scrutiny. Each time of ministry became more covered in prayer to discern when, where, and how we would move. Then about fifteen years into Project Rescue's work we received word that we might have a problem when we next arrived back in Southern Asia. David and

LEADING WITH A WHISPER

I determined that I should go earlier for a friend's meeting, and David would come a couple of days later.

The day after my arrival, I felt an urgency to spend the day in my hotel room praying and seeking God. He led me to a passage in Psalm 18; the words burned from the page:

> I love you, LORD, my strength.
>
> The LORD is my rock, my fortress and my deliverer; my God is my rock, in whom I take refuge, my shield and the horn of my salvation, my stronghold.
>
> I called to the LORD, who is worthy of praise, and I have been saved from my enemies. The cords of death entangled me; the torrents of destruction overwhelmed me. The cords of the grave coiled around me; the snares of death confronted me.
>
> In my distress I called to the LORD; I cried to my God for help. From his temple he heard my voice; my cry came before him, into his ears....
>
> He reached down from on high and took hold of me; he drew me out of deep waters. He rescued me from my powerful enemy, from my foes, who were too strong for me. They confronted me in the day of my disaster, but the LORD was my support. He brought me out into a spacious place; he rescued me because he delighted in me....
>
> To the faithful you show yourself faithful, to the blameless you show yourself blameless, to the pure you show yourself pure, but to the devious you show yourself shrewd. You save the humble but bring low those whose eyes are haughty. You, LORD, keep my lamp burning; my God turns my darkness into light.
>
> —PSALM 18:1–6, 16–19, 25–28

No Turning Back (Reprise)

The next morning when a colleague went with me to pick up David at the international airport, we received word that he had been pulled aside, questioned for a couple of hours, and arrested. Together, we were taken to the police station to await his appearance in court to face unknown charges.

On the way to the court, David and I were taken to a large, government-run hospital so he could have a required physical exam. While he was in the examination room, I was left in a sea of people in the triage area. Countless men and women with babies and little ones surrounded me, standing shoulder to shoulder, all shouting, desperate, and pushing forward, fighting to get help. Many women around me were weeping, clutching their sick babies as they pled with the staff to get medical care.

And while everything was uncertain in that moment for us personally, I looked at the desperate faces of all the people around me. These people were powerless and had little hope or financial means to get help. Mothers were sobbing in despair on behalf of family members who needed critical care. They would never get to the front of the nonexistent line! My heart broke as I silently prayed, "Oh God, with whatever is happening to us, these are the very people for whom David and I have been coming to this nation for thirty-seven years. If there is a cost to pay for it, so be it. We would do it again."

Later, as the arresting officer drove us to court to face the judge and charges, he officiously assured me not to worry. He promised that my husband would get bail and be with me back at the hotel in time for dinner.

But the officer himself was not prepared for what was to come.

When we arrived at the court, it was full of chaos. To both David's amazement and mine a small group of national leader friends in the city had already gotten word of his arrest and were

LEADING WITH A WHISPER

there to meet us. They brought along friends who worked in the legal field to help. These leaders were our brothers and sisters in the best of times and now were willing to be publicly identified with us in the worst of times. We waited with them for David's name to be called; when it was, he was taken to face a very angry judge. An incident had taken place between the United States and this nation just weeks before that publicly and personally shamed a diplomat; when the judge faced David, she was livid because of that incident and happy to publicly shame him since he was an American.

In the clamor I realized justice was being bought and sold in front of our eyes. If God did not intervene on David's behalf, there would be no justice. The judge declared the charges, which were untrue and unbailable. So within seconds, despite lawyers appealing on his behalf, the judge ruled Mr. Grant would be sent to prison to await trial. A lawyer friend standing with me in the back of the courtroom ran me to the front door, where the bailiffs were taking David out to a prison van. She shouted to the guards to stop at the door so I could at least tell my husband goodbye.

We had only seconds, and we were surrounded by guards. I did not know if I would ever see him again.

"David, I love you," I said. "God has given you a gift. Make new friends."

He smiled, and they rushed him away. One of the officers had David's passport, wedding ring, and watch, which he gave to me. As he placed them in my hand, I had a flashback: Thirty-nine years earlier in a hospital emergency room in Wilmington, Delaware, a doctor told me my husband Brian had died. He then placed his wedding ring, watch, and wallet in my hand. Suddenly, a flood of fear inspired by the enemy of our souls rushed over me.

But immediately, just as quickly as that traumatic memory was triggered, it was as if the Spirit of the Lord stood up inside

130

No Turning Back (Reprise)

me and stirred my soul to fight! An anointing to take spiritual authority over fear was immediate. "In the name of Jesus, Satan, I refuse your fear!" I said. "I refuse your lies and your attempt to intimidate! The One who is in David and in me is far greater than you. David's life is in God's hands! I will not be afraid."

God's supernatural presence and peace flooded me. "Father, David is in Your hands," I prayed. "Please give him courage, favor, protection, and wisdom to walk closely with You. Lead him moment by moment by Your Spirit during this unknown time. Cover David with Your peace. In Jesus' mighty name I pray!"

Our friends, my son-in-law, and I slowly walked out of the court together, stunned and wondering what to do next. Out of the corner of my eye I noticed the police officer who brought me and David to court and spent much of the day with us heading toward his van. I ran to him; he looked very uncomfortable.

"Sir, thank you for your kindness to my husband and me today," I said.

He was taken aback. "I just did my job."

"We know," I told him. "But you were also kind to us during a difficult day. Thank you."

And in a moment, that police officer's demeanor changed, and he became emotional. "I'm sorry, Mrs. Grant," he said. "I'm sorry it didn't turn out like I said it would. This is not what usually happens."

"I know, sir." That was all I could say. And with that he walked away, disarmed by grace—just like I have always been too.

For four long days, David was one of twelve thousand men in an infamous prison known for its violence. The battle with fear is not one we fight only once. Sometimes it's a battle we must fight and win one second at a time. And in those four days, I realized how God had so faithfully prepared me once again. He cares.

That first night when I returned to the hotel room without

131

David, my Bible was still open to Psalm 18, lying on what was to have been his pillow beside me. I reread the promises of God that still burned in my heart with life and power. Later that night, through our local friends we learned David was in a cell of seventy men. All slept side by side on mats spread over the concrete floor, and it was winter weather. He was still dressed in his gray flannel slacks, blue shirt, and the navy blazer in which he always traveled; those were all the clothes he had with him, and he was sleeping in them. He definitely stood out.

But David did as David has always done from the time he was a child. He started making new friends from the moment he entered the small cell. Some young men laying around him were weeping over the charges that had brought them into that prison. Some were guilty; some were innocent. Only God knew. But when they heard David was a pastor, they began asking him to pray for them. He would spend much of his time there praying for men who desperately needed help—people he never would have had the opportunity to meet or minister to in his life otherwise.

David's platform was suddenly a prison cell. He drank water from the tin cup a cellmate offered him and ate from his plate. David had nothing. The young men he prayed for began to warn him quietly when he was in danger: "Stay close to us. Those men will hurt you." He witnessed violence but walked in God's peace and grace.

While David was there, our closest national leader friends, our son-in-law, and I spent our days in and around the courts in huddles, working with lawyers and people of influence, interceding intermittently in court hallways for God to make a way for the miracle of David's release. Our friends were making whatever contacts they could with people of influence who might take up David's cause. Unless bail is given, the accused are held in prison until the court case is scheduled and convened. It can

No Turning Back (Reprise)

take years. If convicted, David could have gotten up to five years in prison.

Our nation's embassy was contacting me by phone from the first day. They knew the case already, and each day, they offered to help. But from the first call something in me knew that was not where our help would come from. "Thank you for your offer," I said. "But my husband and I have never come to this nation in a diplomatic capacity. For forty years we have come as friends of this nation. We will trust our friends here to help us."

The embassy staff seemed surprised, but their job was to make that offer. The last day they called me, I said the same thing. This time they acknowledged there was nothing they could have done all along because of the reasons we were in that country. Thankfully, the One who is our help in times of trouble and our local friends were at work the whole time.

One of the days at court, our group of David's friends and family were awaiting another meeting to appeal for bail. A woman approached me and quietly whispered in my ear, "Mrs. Grant, you don't know me, but I'm a pastor's wife. Our people have been praying and trying for years to get permission to have a chaplain visit this prison and minister to prisoners. Permission has never been granted. I'm so sorry this is happening to Brother David. But this is an answer to our prayers. This is the first time we know of that there has been a pastor in that prison praying for prisoners." And with a hug and tears she quickly disappeared back into the maze of courts.

Word had gone out confidentially of David's situation, and our faith family in that nation and back in the United States went to prayer by the thousands. Churches in Southern Asia started around-the-clock prayer meetings, crying out to God for David's release and for the plans of darkness to be defeated. Many reading this book responded to that urgent cry for prayer. Nonstop texts were coming to my phone with specific prayers and words from God that friends received for David and me as the community of faith interceded on the other side of the world. I'll never forget receiving a text from a fifteen-year-old daughter of a pastor in Southern Asia. As she prayed with her family for David, God laid a scripture on her heart to share with us. We cried as we read words that were so clearly from the Lord.

When David was released from prison four days later, the burly bodyguard who accompanied him everywhere by holding his hand (versus making him wear handcuffs) asked to speak to me.

"Mrs. Grant," he said, "in all my years working in this prison, I have never met a man like this man. There is no anger in him, no hatred, no bitterness. Only kindness. He told me about your work with women and children. My daughter is graduating as a social worker. Could she come work with you and your husband?"

Eight days after David's arrest, he was given unconditional bail. Given the circumstances and season, it was a miracle. Fifteen months later we received word that David's case had been dropped. The prosecution's witnesses turned hostile to the prosecution, and it was finished. All glory to God! And so much gratitude went to thousands of family members and friends who stormed heaven in prayer on my husband's behalf day and night. They believed God for a miracle of deliverance. And through it all our Southern Asia family walked with us hour by hour and worked tirelessly for David.

The potential that an obedient yes from God's sons and daughters to His call holds for His kingdom is not determined by the storm. It rests deeply in the love, faithfulness, power, and purposes of the One who calls. God called me to be available to Him to minister wherever, whenever, and however He would

No Turning Back (Reprise)

choose. He simply asked me to trust Him and obey—again and again.

I love the fact that David Grant in prison was the same David Grant he has always been out of prison: an encourager, approachable, available to people, quick to pray—and always with a smile. *No problem!* were and still are two of his favorite words.

And amazingly, he can still find humor in almost anything!

By the time David was sent to prison, both of our daughters were grown and married. They were living in the United States, and both had recently become mothers for the first time to their own children. But it wasn't just those crying babies and midnight feedings that kept them up at night during that ordeal: They were pacing the floors, holding those babies and interceding for David's release the whole time, just as I was.

It was truly a family affair, involving both our natural family and the wider family of God He had given us from around the world.

And when David was released, it was a family celebration and a testament to God's mighty power. We all rejoiced together!

Questions for Reflection

1. Throughout this crisis God's presence, protection, and provision were evident to David and me. What specific promises from Scripture does this story illustrate about God's faithfulness to those who trust Him?

2. After eight days in custody, David miraculously was granted unconditional bail based solely on his word that he would return for trial—despite facing

LEADING WITH A WHISPER

a possible five-year sentence. When we arrived at home, our loved ones were divided on whether we should honor that promise. As a follower of Jesus what key considerations should guide such a decision? What would you have done and why?

3. As the epic battle between good and evil intensifies before Jesus' return, persecution of believers is increasing worldwide. Local pastors and leaders who walked through this situation with us said, "You are showing us how to stand firm. We know our time will come—it's not a matter of *if* but *when*." How can we intentionally prepare ourselves, our families, and the church for trials and suffering as Paul describes in Philippians 3:10? What can leaders do to foster unity and strengthen the church for spiritual battles, rather than allowing division to weaken it?

Dear friends stood faithfully by David and me during his arrest and the challenging months that followed until the case was dropped. We will always be grateful for these brothers and sisters in Christ, who walked closely with us through spiritual battles and celebrated God's ultimate victory, knowing He is forever faithful.

Chapter 12

Lord of Our Seasons

ON MY SIXTIETH birthday I was in South Florida to speak at a women's conference. Some very good friends gave me the gift of a day to myself at one of my favorite places anywhere in the world: the beach on Sanibel Island. So, early in the morning I headed out with my coffee, my Bible, and my journal and found a spot to be alone with God.

When I opened my Bible, I stumbled into a passage I'd never paid too much attention to before. Psalm 92:12–15 reads (emphasis added),

> The righteous will flourish like a palm tree, they will grow like a cedar of Lebanon; planted in the house of the LORD, they will flourish in the courts of our God. *They will still bear fruit in old age, they will stay fresh and green, proclaiming, "The LORD is upright; he is my Rock, and there is no wickedness in him."*

LEADERSHIP HAS SEASONS

As I looked over the watercolor waves, I chuckled out loud. If God had been able to use my life in unexpected ways since I was a teenager, it seemed He could continue to use me and keep me "fresh and green" and fruitful in this new season.

The question was obviously not about God's intent or power to fulfill His Word. It was not whether David and I were still in leadership positions either. It was whether we would continue

Lord of Our Seasons

to stay personally available to the One who had called us as teenagers so many years before. Would we keep walking in prayer and be led by His Spirit for such a time as this?

This could be a flourishing season. I decided to take God at His Word with an expectant heart.

Today, fifteen years later as I am writing this book, David and I are no longer in leadership positions. But because of the gracious new Project Rescue leaders, our daughter, son-in-law, and the board, we remain active founders of that ministry. That means we remain available to serve—doing whatever and going wherever we are most needed. For David that means building relationships, sharing wisdom, and continuing to raise funds on behalf of the ministry God birthed in our hearts. For me it's about continuing to teach and train new leaders and staff across the now sixteen-nation Project Rescue network and ministering on behalf of the organization. We both enjoy being around two very gifted young leaders who are called, passionate, and competent: our own daughter and her precious husband. And when they call us, sometimes a little perplexed by the unexpected challenges of leadership, it's nice to be able to smile and say, "Ah, yes, it's OK. Do you remember when that happened to us too?"

Ever since I was the youth leader at Bethel when I was fifteen, I think I've been more anxious to pass batons to other people than to hold on to them. Perhaps each of us has a natural tendency to either let go early or hold on too long. God has ways of letting us know the time to pass a leadership role to another for a new season, because ministries and people really do have seasons.

But from my experience this is harder for men than women— at least, it has been harder for my husband than for me. For sixty years, David at heart and in calling was a preacher who traveled to churches around the world, ministering and raising

139

funds. Wherever and in whatever season, that was his God-given role and identity. My role changed with distinctive seasons, especially with family. But David and I intentionally made space for each other's individual callings from the beginning of our marriage.

We've tried to be mutually supportive to each other in our different responsibilities and how they interface with God's leading. But David has uniquely done what God impassioned and gifted him to do, with very little change, from the time he was a seventeen-year-old growing up in western Florida to the seventy-nine-year-old missionary statesman and world traveler he is today.

David has been consistent. One pastor's daughter who heard him preach many times as she was growing up summed up his ministry in three points. She told her parents, "Whenever David Grant preaches, he has three basic points: Jesus, Beth, and India!"

But we can be encouraged in our transitions. Stepping away from ministry positions is not relinquishing the privilege of saying yes to God's call and moments of open doors. And I'm so grateful for that. There's still a fire burning in my soul to respond to the nudges of God's still, small voice. We can't just walk away from spiritual battles that must be fought and won. No, in any season, we can continue to lean in to God's promises on behalf of our families, our churches, His kingdom, and a world that deserves the hope Jesus came to give. In our less frantic lives there's now more space for David and me to seek Him, hear His voice, and make ourselves available to engage in His mission as He leads.

What has surprised me in this season is that, over the last five years, God has continued to challenge me to step out in faith in ways that keep stretching me. Recently, David and I had the joy of ministering to eight hundred university students

Lord of Our Seasons

involved in the Chi Alpha campus ministry at a regional West Coast conference convened in Scotts Valley, California. They are literally from all the nations, and we loved being with them. We hoped to somehow share with them out of what God has deposited into our lives. But the students inspired *us* with their passion for God, for seeking Him, and for hearing His heart for their broken world.

God is at work in a younger generation right this minute. We get to affirm their call, pray over them, and share all the God-given wisdom we can. Many (if not most) have not grown up in homes or churches where they had spiritual fathers or spiritual mothers. I've found them to be touched and sincerely grateful when an older person really sees them and cares about how they are doing on their spiritual journeys.

Finally, what a joy it is to watch younger men and women we have walked with and invested in over decades mature and become strong, visionary leaders! They have God-sized vision and take courageous steps of faith in reaping His harvest. The future for the gospel of Jesus reaching people in very difficult places around the world is in some anointed, very capable younger leaders' hands!

Love Has Seasons

Ten years ago David and I were walking and running through an airport concourse together, just as we had for thirty-seven years up to that point. From our first week of marriage, we had learned to walk in step through airports around the world, and it didn't take me long to learn David's gait. Just as clearly as he has his own unique voice, personality, and smile, my husband has always had his own unique way of moving.

But on that day, suddenly I realized David's gait was changing. My heart panicked. Before doctors diagnosed David with

LEADING WITH A WHISPER

Parkinson's disease, which they eventually did in 2015, I knew what was going on because I knew this man's steps, and they were not the same as they had been.

Over time, I've realized I now have two gaits: one that is comfortably mine, and one that I'm still learning to use in order to stay in sync with and supportive of David's changing steps. We have walked and run together for forty-eight years of marriage. Sometimes he prefers for me to walk ahead of him to set the pace and spur him on. More often I try to match his pace. Both of us are still learning in this new season what it means to adapt—one moment and one day at a time.

Recently, the reality struck me that Jesus knows each one of us so personally that if He knows the number of the hairs on our heads, He also knows our gaits. After Jesus' crucifixion, some of His devastated disciples were walking on the road to Emmaus when Jesus literally appeared and walked with them. The just-resurrected Son of God loved His grieving disciples so much—that much!—that He got in step with them and revealed Himself to them. And He does that with us too.

A very old gospel song says, "He walks with me, and He talks with me, and He tells me I am His own." So comfortingly true! I often find myself saying, "Thank You, Jesus, for loving us so much and so personally that You know our very steps and walk with us on the journey in this season."

Other things have changed physically in this new season as well. David's iconic, strong voice is getting softer. So recently, we both agreed to have our hearing checked. We came out from our simultaneous exams and were puzzled to find we had similar results. Two separate doctors asked us if there was any one person in particular we were having a hard time hearing or if it was everyone, and we discovered that the one voice we were both having the hardest time hearing was each other's. So neither one of us needed hearing help yet; we both just needed to put a little more effort into speaking to each other at home. "Just come back next year," the doctors told us.

But some of the things about David Grant that I love the most remain wonderfully the same. He takes boxing lessons with other Parkinson's patients two times a week. And his effect on people in the class every time he arrives is the same one I've watched him have on people all over the world for fifty years: In a gym where many are struggling and few are smiling, David's big grin makes even the most disheartened among them smile. He's the one asking everyone else how it's going. He asks about their families, their children, their ages—and he really cares what the answers are to those questions.

When we first began going there together, I could tell there were some who obviously didn't appreciate David's optimism. They clearly thought he was fake. Plus, when they learned he was a preacher, even though a few were blessed, a few others rolled their eyes.

But now, two years later, everyone there (and their spouses!) has come to love David. He exudes joy, genuine care, and hope. And of course, by now everyone who goes to those boxing sessions has a copy of his new book. Some of them even have two of his books. (You too can find *Born to Give* and *Beyond the Soiled Curtain* at online retailers or through contacting us at projectrescue.com.)

I'm convinced David will go to heaven loving and giving. I want to be like him.

OUR VOICES HAVE SEASONS TOO

David and I remain credentialed ministers with the Peninsular Florida District Council of the Assemblies of God. David began his ministry there as a seventeen-year-old preacher and evangelist. He attended college in Lakeland, Florida, and preached at churches in orange groves and youth camps. His father, Curtis Grant, pastored in Ocala, Florida, while David was growing up, so when we got married, it was an honor for that district and its leadership to become mine as well.

By the time I was ordained for ministry years later, I really had become part of the Peninsular Florida District. In 2009 the gracious nomination for me to step into a newly created role, the first female AG executive presbyter, came from the leadership of the Peninsular Florida District. I've always been grateful they adopted this northern girl into their family.

So it was a privilege when this district leadership team invited me to become the first female to speak at one of its annual ordination services in 2013. It would be my first time to speak for such an occasion as well. I was especially excited because there were a record number of multigenerational female ministers being ordained in that group. It was an honor, and humbling, and I knew I would lose some sleep over that one!

When the day of the Peninsular Florida District ordination services arrived, I had prepared and covered the message in prayer for months. That morning in the hotel room when I needed my quiet time with God, David kindly left it to visit with his many best friends. (They really are!)

But in the middle of my prayers I received a panicked call from our daughter Rebecca. She was there for the conference too, with her husband, Tyler, and their first baby, Judah—who at three months old was going to be dedicated in the service just before I spoke. (That was a touching gift from our district leaders to our whole family.)

But the new "Mimi" in me was torn when our daughter asked me to watch our first grandchild for a couple of hours that morning. I quickly prayed, "Oh, God. I'm trying to pray through and focus on this moment and message! There couldn't be a worse time." But then I heard myself saying, "Sure, it's OK,

Lord of Our Seasons

Becca. No problem." After all, it was baby Judah. And whatever else may have been happening that day, I was his Mimi.

David and I arrived at the very large church that night for the sound check before service, and I was praying for peace. Then, as if on cue, my husband, who has preached more than twenty thousand sermons in his life and can (and sometimes does!) preach in his sleep, tried to be helpful. He started telling me to relax, that it was going to be wonderful, it would all be OK. Just enjoy it!

Then he added, "But make sure you tell some funny stories!"

"Of course, David," I said simply. (I don't even know any funny stories!)

I walked into the almost empty auditorium alone, and a friendly sound-check man asked me to take the platform and mic. "Just say something—anything!" he directed.

So I began to quote Jesus' riveting words from Luke 4:18, "The Spirit of the Lord is on me, because he has anointed me to proclaim good news to the poor. He has sent me to proclaim freedom for the prisoners and recovery of sight for the blind, to set the oppressed free."

As I spoke, God began to stir my spirit once again. His message was like a quickening in my soul. But my voice at the mic was still my voice—quiet and unpredictable.

The sound man released me to go. As I walked down the steps from the platform, a janitor who had been doing some last-minute cleaning in the auditorium approached me kindly and whispered, "Sister, it's going to be OK. I'll be praying for you."

I thanked this brother with a smile and walked away, saying to myself and the Lord, "Yes, Lord, once again, tonight cannot depend on this voice. These people You love, our ministry family, desperately need to hear Your voice! *I will trust You* to speak in power, just as You have promised. You have placed Your words

145

in my mouth for this moment. I trust You to speak through this voice as You have before. When we leave this church tonight, let Your people leave saying, 'We have heard from God!'"

Thankfully, the One who is faithful heard my cry that night along with the district leaders who were calling on Him too. He met us in a powerful way. God's conviction and glory hovered heavily in the room! Many of the women being ordained were touched that night with His Word and His fresh anointing for ministry.

With each season, I have grown to trust God's guidance, His voice, and His power to speak through this very human daughter.

I don't think the fact that God keeps asking us to give Him our frailties, as well as our strengths, for His work ever becomes comfortable. It keeps us on our knees. But our continuing yes to His call in the middle of our weaknesses makes way for His power and anointing to be even more apparent and glorious. As the apostle Paul testified in his letter to the Corinthian church, Jesus told him, "My grace is sufficient for you, for my power is made perfect in weakness" (2 Cor. 12:9).

My new friend, the kind janitor, quickly found me at the end of service and apologized for his words. He was amazed at the power and presence of God that night.

God is faithful still.

No Limits in Jesus

Thankfully, there are no seasons at the feet of Jesus. There are no age barriers when the fire of the Acts 2:4 Pentecost falls. And when the Holy Spirit stirs us as men and women of God, at any age, to speak His words in strategic moments, we still have a treasured opportunity to trust Him and simply use our voices and obey.

Lord of Our Seasons

Until we see Jesus face-to-face, may we remain "fresh and green" in spirit and, in some God-honoring way, flourishing in the work of His kingdom.

QUESTIONS FOR REFLECTION

1. As you reflect on *Leading with a Whisper* as a whole, what truths or insights from our story resonate most with your own walk with God and His unfolding call on your life?

2. At its heart this book is a love story, one of two individuals passionately saying yes to God as a couple through various seasons of life. What areas of strength emerged as David and I obeyed God's call together over the years? Now reflect on your own life—how has saying yes to God shaped your relationships, whether in marriage, family, friendships, or ministry partnerships? What strengths has God cultivated in you and those walking alongside you as you follow His call?

3. Ultimately, this book is the story of every believer. Jesus asks us all to serve Him fully, giving Him both our strengths and our weaknesses in obedience. For me that meant surrendering my physically weakening voice. What challenges is God using in your life to deepen your trust and obedience? Are there fears or limitations that hold you back? Will you dare to trust Him, knowing His strength is made perfect in weakness? Sometimes as we take courageous steps of faith, we find that we have become stronger than we ever imagined because our focus shifts from our own abilities to His matchless presence and power.

LEADING WITH A WHISPER

4. What are the three most important truths or lessons
   you are taking away from this book? Take a moment
   to write them down (where you can find them
   again!). Then in a quiet place welcome His presence,
   seek His guidance, commit these truths to prayer,
   and make them part of your daily walk with God.

LEFT: David and I joyfully joined with family, board members, and friends to pray God's blessing over new Project Rescue leaders Jennifer and Jonathan Barratt in October 2022.

RIGHT: Our granddaughters, Gemma and Maddie Barratt, listened as their Mimi preached. Before the event started, Maddie asked, "Mimi, are you going to preach tonight?" I said, "Yes, Maddie, I am." She replied, "Are you going to dance too?" I said, "Not tonight, Maddie, not tonight."

LEFT: Pastor Stan Grant of Richmond, Virginia, interviewing us about our years of service and God's mission for the church in the future

My mom, Eleanor Oakes, at one hundred years of age is praying over her granddaughter and her grandson-in-law at a Christmas service. She's still a woman of intercession and tender, feisty faith.

Yes, there is still never a dull moment!

Rebecca; her husband, Tyler; and their children (from left), Judah, Ava, and Ella

Jennifer; her husband, Jonathan; and their daughters (from left), Maddie and Gemma

A Personal Invitation to Know Jesus

GOD LOVES YOU deeply. His Word is filled with promises that reveal His desire to bring healing, hope, and abundant life to every area of your being—body, mind, and spirit. More than anything, He wants a personal relationship with you through His Son, Jesus Christ.

If you've never invited Jesus into your life, you can do so right now. It's not about religion—it's about a relationship with the One who knows you completely and loves you unconditionally. If you're ready to take that step, simply pray this prayer with a sincere heart:

> *Lord Jesus, I want to know You as my Savior and Lord. I confess and believe that You are the Son of God and that You died for my sins. I believe You rose from the dead and are alive today. Please forgive me for my sins. I invite You into my heart and my life. Make me new. Help me to walk with You, grow in Your love, and live for You every day. In Jesus' name, amen.*

If you just prayed that prayer, you've made the most important decision of your life. All heaven rejoices with you, and so do I! You are now a child of God, and your journey with Him has just begun. Please contact my publisher at pray4me@charismamedia.com so that we can send you some materials that will help you become established in your relationship with the Lord. We look forward to hearing from you.

Appendix A

Practical Ways to Mentor Children to Act Compassionately Toward Victims of Exploitation

1. Make your children aware of the homeless, those in poverty, and the sexually exploited on your community's streets. Sadly, homelessness, poverty, and sexual exploitation often go hand in hand. Help your children see them as people who were created by God with His image on their lives and created to be redeemed by a loving God. Demonstrate concern and understanding.

2. When you and your children see young girls in public (i.e., malls, streets, parking lots, games) who look highly sexualized at ages eleven to thirteen, don't judge them or use demeaning language. At that age, she's not a predator. But she's possibly a victim at home or of someone close in her life. Demonstrate compassion and kindness.

3. Include your children in your giving to ministries for vulnerable and exploited children and teens. It's an opportunity to grow their awareness of these kinds of injustice and the impact on victims. It also provides an opening to discuss their own vulnerabilities and how to protect themselves from becoming victims on social media or in

LEADING WITH A WHISPER

person. You empower your children to act against evil when they join you in giving to ministries that engage and bring the hope of Jesus to youth without hope. Demonstrate confidence that God will use their contributions too.

4. Do research with your children to discover who is doing something locally to help the homeless, feed the hungry, and intervene on behalf of exploited children in your own city or community. For example, when temperatures drop in your city and the homeless are being served with emergency shelter at reputable organizations like The Salvation Army, do something practical or financial with your children to help. Simple things done quickly in crisis teach your children that it's like Jesus to engage. Jesus came close to the broken. So can we.

5. Lastly, lead your children to pray for the poor, homeless, and sexually exploited as you drive and see them. Prayers don't have to be long or labored. But they can be sincere cries to God on behalf of a stranger who desperately needs Him. Your child's or teenager's prayer at that moment may be the only prayer being prayed—or ever prayed— over that man, woman, girl, or boy. It matters. Demonstrate your belief that God answers prayer.

Appendix B

The Role of Women in Ministry as Described in Holy Scripture

(ADOPTED BY THE GENERAL PRESBYTERY IN SESSION AUGUST 9–11, 2010)

SUPERNATURAL MANIFESTATIONS AND gifts of the Holy Spirit have played a distinctive role in the origin, development, and growth of the Assemblies of God. Since the earliest days of our Fellowship, spiritual gifting has been evident in the ministries of many outstanding women who pioneered and directed a wide spectrum of ministries. It was not uncommon for a married woman to minister in partnership with her husband. Occasionally, husbands worked at secular professions to support the active ministries of their wives. Many women chose to forego marriage to better fulfill the ministries to which the Lord had called them. Courageous women served on mission frontiers at home and abroad as missionaries, evangelists, church planters, pastors, educators, and in other roles.

Pentecostals believe that the outpouring of the Spirit begun in the early twentieth century is a true fulfillment of prophecy: "Your sons and daughters will prophesy....Even on my servants, both men and women, I will pour out my Spirit in those days" (Joel 2:28, 29; cf. Acts 2:16–18). That women as well as men are to prophesy is indicative of their inclusion in the ministries of the new covenant age.

The Bible as Final Authority

While the history and practice of the Assemblies of God appears to demonstrate that God blesses the public ministry of women, debate continues as to the proper role of women in spiritual leadership. Since the Bible is our final authority in all matters of faith and practice, it is important to do a fresh study of its teachings and ensure that our approach is not merely subjective and pragmatic.

It is our intention to examine the biblical text as carefully and objectively as possible, using established rules of exegesis and interpretation. We will note both historical and theological guidance. We will also carefully evaluate texts traditionally used to limit or deny the ministries of women.

Always, it is our intention to be faithful to the teachings of the Bible, God's inspired and infallible Word to humankind. At the same time, we want to be charitable toward those from other traditions who sincerely may disagree with our findings. We recognize that, occasionally, practical compromises in nonessential aspects of ministry practice may be in order to most effectively plant the church in traditionally patriarchal contexts.

Historical and Global Precedent

Historians have observed that in the early days of most revivals, when spiritual fervor is high and the Lord's return is expected at any time, there is often ready acceptance of dynamic, pioneering women ministers. Over time, however, as young churches move toward a more structured ministry, and institutional concerns come to the forefront, the spiritual leadership of women is less readily accepted and church leadership tends to become predominantly male.

The experience of the Assemblies of God has been no exception. Notable women ministers among the early Pentecostals included

The Role of Women in Ministry as Described in Holy Scripture

Maria B. Woodworth-Etter, Aimee Semple McPherson, Alice Reynolds Flower, Anna Ziese, and Marie Burgess Brown. But even though women had great freedom to minister in the early days of the Fellowship, the proportion of women in leadership dropped dramatically beginning in the early 1920s. More recently, the trend is again upward and the number of credentialed women is growing.

Throughout their history, Pentecostals around the world have struggled to apply biblical truth in widely divergent cultural contexts. In some settings, female spiritual leadership is readily accepted; in others, where women have limited ministry, leadership posts are withheld from them. At times there is inconsistency between the leadership a female missionary, for example, has at home and that which she has on the field. There may also be a difference between her ministry opportunities on the field and those of women in the culture she serves. Without doubt, particular cultures have influenced, and continue to influence, the nature and extent of female leadership. While the Church must always be sensitive to cultural concerns, it must nonetheless consistently look to Scripture for principles and directions that rise above particular contextual practices.

BIBLICAL EXAMPLES OF WOMEN IN MINISTRY

Old Testament history includes accounts of strong female leadership in many roles. The following are striking examples: Miriam was a prophet to Israel during the Exodus, alongside her brothers Moses and Aaron (Exodus 15:20). Deborah, both a prophet and a judge, directed Barak to lead the army of Israel into successful combat against Israel's oppressors (Judges 4 to 5). Huldah, also a prophet, authenticated the scroll of the Law

LEADING WITH A WHISPER

found in the temple and helped spark religious reform in the days of Josiah (2 Kings 22:14–20; 2 Chronicles 34:22–28).

The New Testament also shows that women filled important ministry roles in the Early Church. Tabitha (Dorcas) initiated an effective benevolence ministry (Acts 9:36). Philip's four unmarried daughters were recognized prophets (Acts 21:8, 9). Paul singled out two women, Euodia and Syntyche, as "women who have contended at my side in the cause of the gospel, along with Clement and the rest of my fellow workers" (Philippians 4:2, 3). Priscilla was another of Paul's exemplary "fellow workers in Christ Jesus" (Romans 16:3, 4). In Romans 16, Paul greets numerous ministry colleagues, a large number of them women. In these greetings, the word Paul uses to speak of the work (*kopiaō*), or labor, of Mary, Tryphena, Tryphosa, and Persis (Romans 16:6, 12) is one he uses extensively for the labor of ministry (1 Corinthians 16:16; 1 Thessalonians 5:12; 1 Timothy 5:17).

Phoebe, a leader in the church at Cenchrea, was highly commended to the church at Rome by Paul (Romans 16:1, 2). Unfortunately, translation biases have often obscured Phoebe's position of leadership, calling her a "servant" (NIV, NASB, ESV). Yet Phoebe was *diakonos* of the church at Cenchrea. Paul regularly used this term for a minister or leader of a congregation and applied it specifically to Jesus Christ, Tychicus, Epaphras, Timothy, and to his own ministry. Depending on the context, *diakonos* is usually translated "deacon" or "minister." Though some translators have chosen the word deaconess (e.g., RSV, because Phoebe was female), the Greek *diakonos* is a masculine noun. Therefore, it seems likely that *diakonos* was the designation for an official leadership position in the Early Church and the proper translation for Phoebe's role is "deacon" [NIV, NLT, NRSVUE] or "minister."

Moreover, a number of translations reflect similar biases by referring to Phoebe as having been a "great help" (NIV) or "helper"

The Role of Women in Ministry as Described in Holy Scripture

(NASB) of many, including Paul himself (Romans 16:2). The Greek term here is *prostatis*, better translated by the [NRSVUE] as "benefactor" with its overtones of equality and leadership.

Junia was identified by Paul as an apostle (Romans 16:7). Beginning in the thirteenth century, a number of scholars and translators masculinized her name to Junias, apparently unwilling to admit that there was a female apostle. However, the name Junia is found more than 250 times in Rome alone, while the masculine form Junias is unknown in any Greco-Roman source. Paul clearly was a strong advocate of women in ministry.

These instances of women filling leadership roles in the Bible should be taken as a divinely approved pattern, not as exceptions to divine decrees. Even a limited number of women with scripturally commended leadership roles affirm that God does indeed call women to spiritual leadership.

A BIBLICAL SURVEY OF THE ROLE OF WOMEN IN MINISTRY

Of primary importance in defining the scriptural role of women in ministry is the biblical meaning of "ministry." Of Christ our great model, it was said, "For even the Son of Man did not come to be served [*diakoneō*], but to serve [*diakoneō*], and to give his life as a ransom for many" (Mark 10:45; cf. Matthew 20:28). The New Testament leadership modeled by Jesus portrays the spiritual leader as a servant, whether male or female. The question of human authority is not of primary significance, though it naturally arises as organization and structure develop.

Genesis 2:18–25

Some expositors have taught that all women should be subordinate to adult men because Eve was created after Adam to be his "helper" (NIV; "help meet," KJV). Yet the word *ēzer* ("helper") is never used in the Hebrew Bible with a subordinate

LEADING WITH A WHISPER

meaning. Seventeen out of the twenty times it is used, it refers to God as the helper. Eve was created to be a help (*kenegdo*) "suitable" or "corresponding to" Adam, not a subordinate.

Some argue that God created men and women with different characteristics and desires, and that these differences explain why leadership roles should be withheld from women. Others attribute these perceived differences to culture and social expectations imposed on children from birth to adulthood. Physical differences and distinctive biological functions are obvious; but it is only by implication that gender differences can be made to suggest leadership limitations.

PAUL'S EMPHASIS ON CHARISMATIC MINISTRY

Ministry in the New Testament is charismatic in nature. It is made possible and energized as the Holy Spirit sovereignly distributes spiritual gifts (charismata) to each member of the body of Christ (Romans 12:6–8; 1 Corinthians 12:7–11, 27, 28; Ephesians 4:7–12; 1 Peter 4:10–11). While some gifts are a spontaneous work of the Spirit and others are recognized ministry gifts to the Body, all are given for service without regard to gender differentiation. For example, the gift of prophecy is explicitly for both men and women: "Your sons and your daughters will prophesy" (Acts 2:17[, WEB]). The New Testament confirms that women received and exercised this gift of the Spirit (Acts 21:9; 1 Corinthians 11:5).

If Peter found certain statements by Paul hard to understand (2 Peter 3:16), it is no surprise that we, removed by nearly two thousand additional years of history, would share his struggle in interpreting some Pauline passages. While the original audiences were familiar with the problems that Paul addressed, we are left to reconstruct them and apply his prescriptions as best we can in light of the larger context of his letters and biblical

The Role of Women in Ministry as Described in Holy Scripture

revelation. And we, like Peter (2 Peter 3:15), must respect and love our brothers and sisters who hold alternative interpretations on issues that are not critical to our salvation or standing before God. We only request that those interpretations be expressed and practiced in love and consideration for all of God's children, both men and women.

1 Corinthians 11:3–12

The statement that "the man is the head of the woman" has for centuries been used to justify the practice of male superiority and to exclude women from spiritual leadership. Two alternative translations for *kephalē* ("head"), debated widely by contemporary evangelical scholars, are (1) "authority over" and (2) "source" or "origin." Both meanings are found in literature of Paul's time.

Taking the passage as a whole, the second meaning fits as well as or better than the first meaning, leading to the summary statement of verse 12: "As woman came from man, so also man is born of woman. But everything comes from God." Even the relationship between the eternal Son and the Father—"the head of Christ is God" (11:3)—fits better as "source" than "authority over" (cf. John 8:42). Without attempting definitively to resolve this debate, we do not find sufficient evidence in *kephalē* to deny leadership roles to women (in light of biblical examples of women in positions of spiritual authority, and in light of the whole counsel of Scripture).

1 Corinthians 14:34–36

There are only two passages in the entire New Testament that might seem to contain a prohibition against the ministry of women (1 Corinthians 14:34 and 1 Timothy 2:12). Since these must be placed alongside Paul's other statements and practices, they can hardly be absolute, unequivocal prohibitions of the ministry of women. Instead, they seem to be dealing

LEADING WITH A WHISPER

with specific, local problems that needed correction. Therefore, Paul's consistent affirmation of ministering women among his churches must be seen as his true perspective, rather than the apparent prohibitions of these two passages, themselves subject to conflicting interpretation.

There are various interpretations of what Paul was limiting when he said, "Women should remain silent in the churches. They are not allowed to speak" (1 Corinthians 14:34). Paul uses a word to limit the speech of women (*sigatō*) that previously has been used to limit the speech of those speaking in tongues if there is no interpretation (1 Corinthians 14:28) and prophets if a prophecy is given to another person (v. 30). It is only under such specific circumstances that the speech of tongues speakers, prophets, and women are to be silenced in the church. Under what circumstances then, is the speech of women to be limited?

Options include (1) chatter in public services, (2) ecstatic disruptions, (3) certain authoritative ministries (such as judging prophecies), and (4) asking questions during the service. It is apparent that Paul permitted women both to pray and prophesy in public worship at Corinth (1 Corinthians 11:5). Moreover, Paul advised that those who prophesy (evidently including women) should be among the ones to judge prophecies (1 Corinthians 14:29). Therefore, as with Paul's constraints on both men and women tongues speakers and prophets, it may be that Paul's additional constraints on women have to do with other forms of disruptive speech.

While the precise nature of Paul's prohibition in this text is a matter of ongoing study, we do conclude that it does not prohibit female leadership, but like the rest of the chapter, it admonishes that "everything should be done in a fitting and orderly way" (1 Corinthians 14:40).

The Role of Women in Ministry as Described in Holy Scripture

1 Timothy 2:11–15

The meaning and application of Paul's statement, "I do not permit a woman to teach or to have authority over a man; she must be silent" (1 Timothy 2:12), have puzzled interpreters and resulted in a variety of positions on the role of women in ministry and spiritual leadership.

From the above survey of passages on exemplary women in ministry, it is clear that Paul recognized the ministry of women. There were obvious problems in Ephesus, some relating to women. Some women were evidently given to immodest apparel and adornment (1 Timothy 2:9). The younger widows were "into the habit of being idle....And not only do they become idlers, but also gossips and busybodies, saying things they ought not to" (1 Timothy 5:13). In his second letter to Timothy, Paul warned against depraved persons (possibly including women) who manipulated "weak-willed," or "gullible" women (2 Timothy 3:6[, NIV, WEB]).

A reading of the entire passage of 1 Timothy 2:9–15 strongly suggests that Paul was giving Timothy advice about dealing with some heretical teachings and practices specifically involving women in the church at Ephesus. The heresy may have been so serious that he had to say about the Ephesian women, "I am not allowing women to teach or have authority over a man." Other passages show that such exclusion was not normative in Paul's ministry.

1 Timothy 3:1–13

This entire passage has been held by some to confirm that all leaders and authorities in the Early Church were supposed to be males. The passage deals primarily with male leadership, most likely because of majority practice and expectations. But there is also significant support for female leadership.

Typical of modern English versions, the New International

LEADING WITH A WHISPER

Version translates verse 11, "In the same way, their wives are to be women worthy of respect." The NIV translators arbitrarily decided that the verse refers to the wives of deacons (even though there is no reference in the preceding qualifications of elders to their wives).

However, the word translated "wives" is the plural of the Greek word *gynē* which can be translated as either "woman" or "wife" depending on the context. Recognizing this, the NIV translators did include the word "deaconesses" as an alternate reading in their footnotes. But the NASB and the [NRSVUE] render the plural form of *gynē* as "women." Thus, literally, the verse is addressing the qualifications of women in spiritual leadership who, in this context, might easily be called "deacons."

Although the first-century cultural milieu produced a primarily male church leadership, this passage along with other biblical evidence of female spiritual leadership (e.g., Acts 21:9; Romans 16:1–15; Philippians 4:2, 3) demonstrates that female leadership was not prohibited, either for Paul's day or for today. Passages that imply most leaders were male may not be taken to say that all leaders were male, since the biblical record speaks approvingly of numerous female leaders.

Galatians 3:28

Those who oppose allowing women to hold positions of spiritual leadership place contextual limitations on Galatians 3:28, "There is neither Jew nor Greek, slave nor free, male nor female, for you are all one in Christ Jesus."

Some interpreters restrict the meaning of this triad to salvation by faith or oneness in Christ. That truth is certainly articulated throughout Scripture. Yet the verse carries a ring of universal application for all our relationships, not just an assurance that anyone can come to Christ. "Neither Jew nor Greek, slave nor

The Role of Women in Ministry as Described in Holy Scripture

free, male nor female"—these are basic relationship principles to which faithful followers of Christ must give highest priority.

The God of the Bible "does not show favoritism" (Romans 2:11; cf. also 2 Samuel 14:14; 2 Chronicles 19:7; Acts 10:34; Ephesians 6:9). He calls whom He will and gives gifts and ministries as He chooses; humans must not put limitations on divine prerogatives. The strained relationship between Adam and Eve, including the statement that "he will rule over you" (Genesis 3:16), comes as a result of the curse, making it clear that this was not a part of God's original and durable design for humankind. In Christ we are truly set free from sin and its curse, which separate us from God and each other and cause us to elevate or demean according to race, social standing, or gender.

THEREFORE, WE CONCLUDE

After examining the various translations and interpretations of biblical passages relating to the role of women in the first-century church, and desiring to apply biblical principles to contemporary church practice, we conclude that we cannot find convincing evidence that the ministry of women is restricted according to some sacred or immutable principle.

We are aware that the ministry and leadership of women are not accepted by some individuals, both within and outside the Christian community. We condemn all prejudice and self-promotion, by men or women. The existence of bigotry against women in our world, and all too often in the church, cannot be denied. But there is no place for such an attitude in the body of Christ. We acknowledge that attitudes of secular society, based on long-standing practice and tradition, have influenced the application of biblical principles to local circumstances. We desire wisely to respect yet help redeem cultures that are at variance with Kingdom principles. Like Paul, we affirm that the

Great Commission takes priority over every other consideration. We must reach men and women for Christ, no matter what their cultural or ethnic customs may be. The message of redemption has been carried to remote parts of the world through the ministry of dedicated, Spirit-filled men and women. A believer's gifts and anointing should still today make a way for his or her ministry. The Pentecostal ministry is not a profession to which men or women merely aspire; it must always be a divine calling, confirmed by the Spirit with a special gifting.

The Assemblies of God has been blessed and must continue to be blessed by the ministry of God's gifted and commissioned daughters. The Bible repeatedly affirms that God pours out His Spirit upon both men and women and thereby gifts both sexes for ministry in His Church. Therefore, we must continue to affirm the gifts of women in ministry and spiritual leadership.

Surely, the enormous challenge of the Great Commission to "go and make disciples of all nations" (Matthew 28:19) requires the full deployment of all God's Spirit-gifted ministers, both men and women.[1]

Appendix C

Recommended Reading List

THESE ARE SOME of my favorite resources from different seasons.

- Baillie, John. *A Diary of Private Prayer: A Devotional Classic.* Fireside, 1996.

- Bradford, James T. *Lead So Others Can Follow.* Salubris Resources, 2015.

- Brother Lawrence. *The Practice of the Presence of God with Spiritual Maxims.* Revell, 1967.

- Christian, Jayakumar. *God of the Empty-Handed: Poverty, Power, and the Kingdom of God.* MARC Books, 1999.

- Corbett, Steve, and Brian Fikkert. *When Helping Hurts: Alleviating Poverty Without Hurting the Poor...and Yourself, Revised Edition.* Moody Publishers, 2012.

- Elmer, Duane. *Cross-Cultural Servanthood: Serving the World in Christlike Humility.* InterVarsity Press, 2006.

- Fee, Gordon D. *Listening to the Spirit in the Text.* William Eerdmans Publishing Company, 2000.

- Georges, Jayson, and Mark D. Baker. *Ministering in Honor-Shame Cultures.* IVP Academic, 2016.

- Gill, Deborah M., and Barbara Cavaness. *God's Women Then and Now*. Grace and Truth, 2004.

- Girdler, Joseph S., and Carolyn Tennant. *Keys to the Apostolic and Prophetic: Embracing the Authentic—Avoiding the Bizarre*. Meadow Stream Publishing, 2019.

- Kendall, R. T. *The Anointing: Yesterday, Today, Tomorrow*. Charisma House, 2003.

- Kendall, R. T. *Total Forgiveness*. Charisma House, 2007.

- Kilbourn, Phyllis, and Marjorie McDermid, eds. *Sexually Exploited Children: Working to Protect and Heal*. MARC Books, 1998.

- Langberg, Diane. *Suffering and the Heart of God: How Trauma Destroys and Christ Restores*. New Growth Press, 2015.

- Lingenfelter, Judith E., and Sherwood G. Lingenfelter. *Teaching Cross-Culturally: An Incarnational Model for Learning and Teaching*. Baker Academic, 2003.

- Lingenfelter, Sherwood. *Transforming Culture: A Challenge for Christian Mission*. Baker Books, 1998. See the reference in my book in chapter 7, "Harems, Servant Leaders, and Little Kings"; Lingenfelter's concept of culture as a "prison of disobedience" is found on pages 18–20.

- Markandaya, Kamala. *Nectar in a Sieve*. Signet Classics, 2010. The book is a classic story of an Indian woman's life journey in a traditional rural

Recommended Reading List

village. This little book was handed to me by a colleague soon after I arrived in the country to gain insight into the lives of India's daughters.

- Mernissi, Fatema. *Scheherazade Goes West: Different Cultures, Different Harems.* Washington Square Press, 2001.

- Meyers, Bryant L. *Walking with the Poor: Principles and Practices of Transformational Development.* Orbis Books, 2003.

- Moore, Shayne, Sandra Morgan, and Kimberly McOwen Yim. *Ending Human Trafficking: A Handbook of Strategies for the Church Today.* InterVarsity Press, 2022.

- Palmer, Parker J. *The Courage to Teach: Exploring the Inner Landscape of a Teacher's Life.* Jossey-Bass, 1998.

- Plueddemann, James E. *Leading Across Cultures: Effective Ministry and Mission in the Global Church.* InterVarsity Press, 2009.

- Qualls, Joy E. A. *God Forgive Us for Being Women: Rhetoric, Theology, and the Pentecostal Tradition.* Pickwick Publications, 2018.

- Robb, Ruth H., and Marion L. S. Carson. *Walk into Freedom: Christian Outreach to People Involved in Commercial Sexual Exploitation.* The People's Seminary Press, 2020.

- Runcorn, David. *A Center of Quiet: Hearing God When Life Is Noisy.* InterVarsity Press, 1990.

- Satyavrata, Ivan. *Pentecostals and the Poor: Reflections from the Indian Context.* Asia Pacific Theological Seminary Press, 2017.

- Tennant, Carolyn. *Catch the Wind of the Spirit: How the Five Ministry Gifts Can Transform Your Church.* Meadow Stream Publishing, 2022.

- Volf, Miroslav. *Free of Charge: Giving and Forgiving in a Culture Stripped of Grace.* Zondervan, 2005.

- Wood, George O., James T. Bradford, and Beth Grant. "The Best Is Yet to Come: Why Credentialed Women Ministers Matter to the Assemblies of God." *Enrichment*, Spring 2015. https://enrichmentjournal.ag.org/Issues/2015/Spring-2015/The-Best-Is-Yet-to-Come.

Notes

CHAPTER 7

1. Robert L. Welsch and Luis A. Vivanco, "Cultural Anthropology: Chapter Outline," *Oxford University Press*, accessed March 26, 2025, https://global.oup.com/us/companion.websites/9780199925728/stud/ch10/outline/#:~:text=For%20anthropologists%2C%20politics%20is%20not,violence%2C%20and%20control%20over%20resources.
2. Sherwood Lingenfelter, *Transforming Culture: A Challenge for Christian Mission* (Baker Books, 1998), 18–20.

CHAPTER 9

1. George O. Wood et al., "The Best Is Yet to Come: Why Credentialed Women Ministers Matter to the Assemblies of God," *Enrichment,* accessed April 9, 2025, https://enrichmentjournal.ag.org/Issues/2015/Spring-2015/The-Best-Is-Yet-to-Come.
2. Darrin J. Rodgers, "Fully Committed: One Hundred Years of the Assemblies of God," *Assemblies of God Heritage*, accessed April 9, 2025, https://ifphc.org/About/AG-History.
3. Joann Butrin, "The Woman in the Room: Working Together in Ministry Should Be Normal, Not Weird," *Influence*, November 15, 2023, https://influencemagazine.com/Practice/The-Woman-in-the-Room.
4. Kristel Zelaya, "Pathfinder: Equipping Women to Serve in Ministry," AG News, March 5, 2025, https://news.ag.org/en/articles/news/2025/02/pathfinder-equipping-women-to-serve-in-ministry#:~:text=And%20with%2011%2C046%20women%20currently,for%20the%20ones%20coming%20behind; "We Are NWM," Assemblies of God Network of Women Ministers,

accessed April 15, 2025, https://www.womenministers.ag.org/.

CHAPTER 10

1. "Study Determining Whether Women Truly Talk More Than Men," University of Arizona, updated February 6, 2025, https://psychology.arizona.edu/news/study-determining-whether-women-truly-talk-more-men.

APPENDIX B

1. "The Role of Women in Ministry," Assemblies of God, accessed April 10, 2025, https://ag.org/-/media/AGORG/Beliefs/Position-Papers/PP_The_Role_of_Women_in_Ministry.pdf. Reprinted with permission. Scripture references are from the 1984 version of the NIV.

Acknowledgments

OVER THE YEARS as I've ministered in very diverse settings, I've found those listening to be gracious and sincere in their responses. But one pattern has emerged. Depending on the setting, culture, and generation, listeners were not always sure what to call what they just heard. "Dr. Beth, I loved your, um, speech!" Or maybe, "Your sermon?" Message? Lecture? I've always smiled and been sympathetic as they looked for a term. They just knew that God touched them and spoke through what they heard. And I've been supportive because in many moments of ministry, I wasn't quite sure what to call my presentation either. What mattered most was that God faithfully put His words in my mouth, we heard from God, and He was at work among us through His Word and by His Spirit.

So I sign off on this manuscript at peace knowing that you, reader, may not be sure what to call *Leading with a Whisper* either. I know that what was a dream tucked away decades ago, waiting for the right time, became God's assignment to prayerfully sit down, write the things He had done, and share His all-sufficient grace on my journey. And once again, God at work cannot be captured by our terminology. We can only tell the story faithfully, see His hand at work, and be sensitive to the wind of His Spirit blowing. And that is enough. The Holy Spirit personalizes the story for each reader whose heart is seeking Him. He knows what we need. I am ever grateful.

With that in mind, I'm indebted to David's and my friend Stephen Strang, founder of Charisma Media, and to the team of editors at Charisma House. They worked with me when I couldn't yet totally describe what this book would look like. And in the process, as direction grew with God's help, they brought

LEADING WITH A WHISPER

their excellent professional skills around the emerging story to bring *Leading with a Whisper* to completion. That's a wonderful gift.

No dream from God can be accomplished without the practical, willing hands of those who work with us to make it happen. My special thanks go to our Project Rescue leadership and US Resource Office team, who were available and supportive. My husband's administrative assistant, Jewell Woodward, was especially helpful to me in communicating with all involved in the story and in helping find photos from over sixty years! She's professional, efficient, and always a joyful team member— whatever the task.

So many of our Assemblies of God World Missions leaders, colleagues, and international and US church partners have been part of my story as well as David's. In many ways, the stories woven through *Leading with a Whisper* are theirs too. Over decades, it's been a privilege to walk together and fulfill God's great mission as a team. This calling and its fulfillment have always been accomplished side by side for God's glory.

Special thanks go to my mom, Eleanor Oakes, who is now 101 years old and has prayed for me and over the process of writing this book every day since I began. Her eyesight is almost gone now. We will sit together, and I will read this story to her. She can't wait!

My great thanks go to our daughters, Rebecca Shults and Jennifer Barratt, for walking this writing journey with me. In the process they learned parts of my story they had never heard before—some sober, some funny, some ordinary, and hopefully, some inspiring. As I tried to find words for things I had never put in writing before, Rebecca and Jennifer would take me on a ride with a cup of coffee out into the country.

I discovered in the middle of writing that there was a spiritual battle I had to personally press through. Why was I surprised?

174

Acknowledgments

Nothing worth doing for God that is in any way healing, redeeming, releasing, and God honoring comes without push-back from His archenemy. Our daughters were always just a text away and believed this story should be shared. And they were the ones who came up with the wonderfully fitting title, *Leading with a Whisper.*

Lastly, I want to acknowledge with much love and appreciation my husband, David, and his enthusiastic support for this endeavor. He loves books, he loves his books, and he will love mine too. Thank you, David Lowell Grant! You are amazing. I love you.

About the Author

BETH GRANT, PHD, began vocational ministry at age twenty-four and became a credentialed minister with the Assemblies of God a year later while serving as a minister of music and education in Wilmington, Delaware. A week after marrying her husband, missionary David Grant, she began what would become a life journey of serving in theological education, ministry to women called to ministry, and cross-cultural leadership in Southern Asia, Europe, and the US.

In 1997 Grant and her husband pioneered Project Rescue, a compassionate, transformational ministry to prostituted women and children in red-light districts in Southern Asia. Since then, Project Rescue and its global partners in other regions have grown and been on the front lines of rescuing and restoring exploited women and children in thirty-eight cities in sixteen nations through best practices and the love and power of God. Grant's focus on cross-cultural education and training was implemented in partnership with the Faith Alliance Against Slavery and Trafficking (FAAST) to produce their first faith-based curriculum, "Hands that Heal: International Curriculum to Train Caregivers of Trafficking Survivors" (2007). Her book *Courageous Compassion: Confronting Social Injustice God's Way* (2014) is a call to the global church to live out the compassionate, life-changing mission of Jesus for the most vulnerable victims of injustice in our world—in places where the hope of Jesus is most needed.

Beth Grant was elected to serve the Assemblies of God USA denomination as its first female executive presbyter in 2009, where she served until 2023. Over several decades teaching in seminaries, Christian colleges, and women's conferences in India,

About the Author

Europe, and the US, she has become recognized as a passionate voice for young women who are called by God to ministry, urging them to recognize that call, trust the One who calls, and step out in obedience, in faith, and in the power of His Spirit.

Beth Grant earned a PhD in intercultural education from Biola University in La Mirada, California, and an MA in cultural anthropology from the Assemblies of God Theological Seminary in Springfield, Missouri.

Along with her husband, David, Grant continues to travel on behalf of Project Rescue, as both of them are active founders, and personally on behalf of empowering women in ministry and leadership. She loves being a mom to her daughters, Rebecca and Jennifer, and a mother-in-law to Tyler Shults and Jonathan Barratt (all of whom now serve with Project Rescue). She delights in being "Mimi" to Judah, Ella, and Ava Shults and to Gemma and Maddie Barratt.

Contact Us

PROJECT RESCUE

www.projectrescue.com
info@projectrescue.com
417-833-5564

Project Rescue
PO Box 922
Springfield, MO 65801

RESCUE & RESTORE
CERTIFICATE PROGRAM • MINISTRY TO THE SEXUALLY EXPLOITED

Rescue & Restore exists to train individuals and equip churches to minister to those who have been sexually exploited so that they might find dignity, healing, and a new life through a relationship with God.

Learn more
www.projectrescue.com/certificate